JELLY'S
LAST JAM

JELLY'S LAST JAM

BOOK AND DIRECTION BY

George C. Wolfe

LYRICS BY

Susan Birkenhead

MUSIC BY

Jelly Roll Morton

ADDITIONAL MUSIC &
MUSICAL ADAPTATION BY

Luther Henderson

INTRODUCTION BY

John Lahr

Theatre Communications Group
1993

Wolfe, George C.
Jelly's last jam / book by George C. Wolfe ; lyrics by Susan Birkenhead.—
1st ed.
ISBN 1-55936-068-2 (cloth)—ISBN 1-55936-069-0 (paper)
1. Morton, Jelly Roll, d. 1941—Drama.   2. Jazz musicians—United States—Drama.
I. Birkenhead, Susan. II. Title.
PS3573.05213J45 1993
812'.54—dc20   92-44018
CIP

Book design and composition by The Sarabande Press

First Edition, July 1993

CONTENTS

INTRODUCTION

BY JOHN LAHR

When you're talking about the American musical, you're talking Broadway religion: the salvation of applause, the beatification of the bottom line, the gospel of good times. This faith has been sorely tested over the last generation, and the musical has gone into the wilderness. What America is the new musical singing about? Vietnam put paid to legends of abundance and righteousness which were formerly the musical's manifest destiny. The musical lost confidence in its content, its form, its audience, and its country. German fairytales, French *pointillism*, Victorian England, '30s Berlin—many of the most celebrated recent musicals seem prepared to sing about anything but America. In the heyday of America's world power, musicals gave the society legends of triumph; now in the society's retreat from power, the musical is making legends of collapse. The musical was fun before it was art; but give or take a few blips of buoyancy (*Hair, A Chorus Line, Chicago*), anxiety has become the new abundance. The musical, like the winded culture it reflects, seems at a loss to know what or how to celebrate. Pluck 'n loathing has replaced pluck 'n luck as the prevailing credo, the delirium of hope giving way to the delirium of despair. "The more he bleeds, the more he lives/he never forgets and he never forgives," chants the chorus about the Demon Barber of Fleet Street in Stephen Sondheim's masterpiece *Sweeney Todd*. The lines could be the epitaph of the blasted hopes and lucid doubts that the paying customers have been asked to applaud in these wilderness years where joy has been banished from the contemporary musical's definition of maturity.

But joy and irony—the adult acknowledgement of liberation *and* limitation, blessing *and* barbarity—can exist on stage as they do in life, and *Jelly's Last Jam* has arrived to show Broadway how to be at once pertinent and populist, kinetic and not camp. The show is a watershed, engineered by its playwright/director George C. Wolfe and an extraordinary array of theatrical talent. The fact that this is Mr. Wolfe's first Broadway play, his first Broadway libretto, and his first shot at directing a Broadway musical is a kind of show-biz miracle in itself. But the real significance of the occasion is the redemption that *Jelly's Last Jam* holds out for the future of the American musical, whose audiences seem to get smaller as its songs get "smarter." The show opens the musical up to new mythologies, new aesthetics and a new historical sophistication. The message behind the musical as well as Jelly Roll Morton's songs is spelled out for the audience by a character called Jack the Bear. Says The Bear: "High life or no life, ya still gotta live yo' life." That's news to Broadway, whose celebration of the good life has rarely included ordinary life.

"What I've been trying to evolve is a visual and emotional vocabulary which is as evocative and as subliminally powerful as black music," says Wolfe, who writes the blues with words, images and music. The blues are irony in action; in them, the contradictions of hurt and happiness coalesce. *Jelly's Last Jam* walks it like it talks it. "To relive your past without pain is a lie," says The Chimney Man, the *deus ex machina* in this all-singing, all-dancing Last Judgement, as he indicts Jelly Roll Morton for a moral amnesia that mirrors the commercial musical's practice of removing pain for gain. *Jelly's Last Jam* shows what it means to properly stimulate an audience instead of tickling it to death. "The conventional Broadway wisdom is 'When in doubt give 'em spectacle,'" says Wolfe. "But a human being going through emotions is the best sort of event you can witness."

The first of many accomplishments of *Jelly's Last Jam* is to raise the amperage of passion and to sanctify the moment. In *Jelly's Last Jam*, the audience cheers a New Orleans belter called Miss Mamie whose "story lasted 'bout as long as my song," when she concludes "Michigan Water," singing "So all you gumbo-eatin' bitches, can kiss my ass goodbye!" The song is an exhibition of being: slangy, sensuous and sensational. The defiance in Miss Mamie's voice echoes the defiance in *Jelly's Last Jam* which wants a mass communication but, unlike the influential musicals of Sondheim and his imitators, doesn't disdain the mass. The show, like Miss Mamie's blues, thrills an audience by bending the musical's structure to assert its gorgeous authenticity. *Jelly's Last Jam* is talking about surviving the society's sins, and the American musical can kiss nostalgia and deconstruction goodbye.

Jelly's Last Jam returns character to the concept musical which all too often has become a song cycle where a few strokes of personal idiosyncrasy pass for characterization. A smart lyric in the mouth of a stick-figure is a theatrical Nothingburger. This mutation has robbed the musical of an essential playfulness and penetration. Atrophy has been declared art and, instead of being a game of show and tell, the musical has become a song-heavy game of tell and tell. *Jelly's Last Jam* redresses some of this narrative imbalance. The cunning lyrics of Susan Birkenhead make an event of plot and personality, and not her brilliance. Luther Henderson's low-down, sumptuous jazz score, inspired by Jelly Roll's music, punches out the subtext of Birkenhead's tasty words with bold strokes whose dissonances invoke the black American jook and not the European avant-garde. The show brings rambunctiousness and noise and a sense of lived-life back to Broadway. If the standing ovations *Jelly's Last Jam* received when I saw it in New York and in Los Angeles (where it was the highest grossing show in the Mark Taper Forum's twenty-five-year history) are accurate barometers, *Jelly's Last Jam* has finally found a sophisticated way of retrieving the modern musical from the respectable hush of museum theatre and returning it to the rousing hubbub of the mass from which the form's power springs.

Wolfe is a folklorist, and his vivacious characters exude the high definition and the high style of self-contained, un-oppressed denizens of a black world. The paradoxical Jelly Roll Morton, the self-proclaimed Creole "inventor of jazz" and a traitor to his race, is the central raffish figure whose racism the musical controversially debates, but there are others: Jack the Bear, Foot-in-Your-Ass-Sam, Too-Tight Nora, Three-Finger Jake, Sweet Anita, The Hunnies who capture a variety of moments, moods and styles of black life as the story of jazz works its way with Jelly Roll from New Orleans to Chicago and to New York. These characters revel in their power and in their prowess. "I try to write characters with an outrageous sense of self because, in their presence, they're the opposite of oppressed," says Wolfe. "I love people who carry their power with them. It's one of my theories that black folks carry all of their stuff with them all the time because they didn't have time to pack the first time around. They don't keep their arrogance, their humility, their anger, their passion locked in little boxes. So that the next time, if somebody tries to take it away, they'll have it *all* with them."

The first black Broadway musical, Noble Sissle and Eubie Blake's *Shuffle Along* (1920), made it to Broadway by pandering, as its title suggests, to downtown racial stereotypes. Nothing too much has changed over the years until *Jelly's Last Jam*. A number of black shows from *Ain't Misbehavin'* to *Bubbling Brown Sugar* to *Five Guys Named Moe* have brought black music and black talent to Broadway but refused to put the ravishing energy in a proper historical context. The shows are another form of shucking, what Wolfe calls "cultural strip mining," that robs black expression both of context and of ideas. Wolfe's chilling Act One finale, "Dr. Jazz," makes a spectacle of this denial. In blackface and bellhop caps, the chorus struts the fun-loving racist stereotype behind Jelly as he sings about the delightful spell of his music whose syncopation is meant to make the public forgive and forget the sin that made it and his own transparent shortcomings.

LISTEN PEOPLE HERE COMES DOCTOR JAZZ
HE'S GOT GLORY ALL AROUND HIM, YES HE HAS
WHEN THE WORLD GOES WRONG
N' YOU GOT THE BLUES
HE'S THE MAN WHAT MAKES YOU GET OUT
BOTH YOUR DANCIN' SHOES . . .

In *Jelly's Last Jam*, Wolfe is not reflecting a white world but debating a black one. He celebrates Afro-American culture not as a sociological problem, but as a way of being.

"Every phase of Negro life is highly dramatized," wrote Zora Neale Hurston whom Wolfe successfully adapted for the stage in *Spunk* and whose famous essay *Characteristics of Negro Expression* is gospel to Wolfe. "There is an impromptu ceremony always ready for every hour of life. No little moment passes unadorned. Whatever the Negro does of his own volition, he embellishes." The Afro-American will to adorn glories in survival and the ability of the race to reinterpret white civilization for its own use. The stylishness of *Jelly's Last Jam* is witness to the originality and the ever-changing energy of the black aesthetic. Morton's jazz motifs decorate the melodic line of his songs, tap dancing decorates motion, and the trio of Hunnies with legs up to their armpits decorate just about everything else. From the sinking of a pool ball to the slamming of a door to the recreation of the L.A. landscape (a couple of upstage zigzag lines of neon), Wolfe's visual language misses no opportunity for startling invention. The asymmetry and angularity of Wolfe's stage pictures, which make the musical dynamic and fresh, are also part of the black aesthetic. "There's a tribe in Africa that ploughs its fields in perfect squares but leaves one square that isn't perfect," explains Wolfe. "It's *embracing* the imperfection as opposed to being *haunted* by it."

Jelly's Last Jam also reclaims the gorgeous power of tap dancing as part of musical story-telling. Jelly Roll Morton was a piano player not a tap dancer; but in Wolfe's script, tap becomes a percussive beat which is at the root of the rhythm and the anger. In fact, the tap dancing begins when Young Jelly learns syncopation from the cries of New Orleans street vendors as the Root Man shouts "roots, roots, roots," and soon launches into a show-stopping tap competition with Jelly. "Simply because a silhouette is deemed offensive," says Wolfe of the reactionary overtones of tap, "you don't throw away the silhouette or the content, you reclaim it." And so he has: tap becomes a metaphor of Jelly Roll's frustration as well as creation. It's awesome to watch.

Wolfe's story turns the table on the imperialism of self which Broadway musicals and its stars have traditionally made glorious. In this time of riot and recession, *Jelly's Last Jam* sounds a new note on the Broadway musical stage. The show dramatizes "destiny of me" being transformed into the destiny of *we*. This is also news. "When you're dependent on those around you in order to survive, you negotiate a sense of the collective, you evolve this sense of 'we,'" says Wolfe. Jelly Roll learns finally

that he's the messenger, not the message. Sings the ensemble at
the finale:

> ALL THE LOVIN'
> THE LEAVIN'
> THE LOSIN'
> WHO WE ARE
> AND WHAT WE USED TO BE
> IT'S IN THE MUSIC
> PLAY THE MUSIC FOR ME . . .

Jelly Roll's music expresses the stories of people we'll never
know; but *Jelly's Last Jam* dramatizes the sin of separation that
we know all too well. Jelly abandons the mythology of individ-
ualism to embrace the new mythology of community, which puts
the show at the spiritual center of the American moment. "Go
forth Armstrong! Go forth Ellington! Go forth Basie, Bolden, n'
Bechet," says the Chimney Man. "Go forth Morton!" A door
festooned with African hieroglyphs opens, and Jelly Roll passes
through it into history. But history is fable agreed up. And *Jelly's
Last Jam* astutely renegotiates the audience's idea of black culture and the nature of the musical itself. It's a tremendous
imaginative feat, and a tremendous show, and a tremendous step
in the right direction for an art form which, like the society itself,
has lost touch with the best part of itself.

PRODUCTION HISTORY

Jelly's Last Jam was commissioned by Margo Lion and Pamela Koslow-Hines.

It was developed under the auspices of the Mark Taper Forum in Los Angeles (Gordon Davidson, Artistic Director) and received its world premiere there on February 24, 1991 with the official press opening on March 7. The production closed on April 21.

George C. Wolfe directed the following cast:

Jelly Roll Morton.......................Obba Babatunde
Chimney Man..............................Keith David
The Hunnies ....Phylliss Bailey, Patty Holley, Regina Le Vert
His Women
    Maman..............................Karole Foreman
    Gran Mimi ....Freda Payne
    Anita...............................Tonya Pinkins
    Mabel ....Leilani Jones
His Past
    Young Jelly......................Robert Barry Fleming
    Eulalie ....Peggy Blow
    Viola ....Phylliss Bailey

Amede . . . . .Patty Holley
The Ancestors . . . . .Timothy Smith, Mary Bond Davis,
          Patrick McCollum, Peggy Blow, Gil Pritchett III
Buddy Bolden . . . . .Ruben Santiago-Hudson
Blues Singer. . . . . .Mary Bond Davis
Three-Finger Jake . . . . .Gil Pritchett III
Too-Tight Nora. . . . . .Deborah L. Sharpe
Jack the Bear. .Stanley Wayne Mathis
Hick Man. . . . . .Gil Pritchett III
Hick Woman . . . . .Regina Le Vert
Grieving Widow. . . . . .Patty Holley
Dead Man. . . . . .Jerry M. Hawkins
Pool Player . . . . .Patrick McCollum
Melrose Brothers, Agents, Gangsters. . . . . .Jerry M. Hawkins,
                                            Timothy Smith
The Crowd: Peggy Blow, Mary Bond Davis, Robert Barry
    Fleming, Karole Foreman, Jerry M. Hawkins, Stanley Wayne
    Mathis, Patrick McCollum, Freda Payne, Tonya Pinkins, Gil
    Pritchett III, Ruben Santiago-Hudson, Deborah L. Sharpe,
    Timothy Smith
Loose Lil and the Jungle Inn Jammers: Linda Twine, Garnett
    Brown, Richard Grant, Jeffery Clayton, Quentin Dennard,
    Karl Vincent

George Tsypin designed the set; Toni-Leslie James, the costumes;
James F. Ingalls, the lighting; Hope Clarke was the choreographer; Linda Twine was the musical director; Mary K. Klinger
was the production stage manager; Corey Beth Madden was the
associate producer; Randall Sommer was the assistant to George
C. Wolfe.

In November 1991 a revised version of the musical received a
workshop. Gregory Hines played the role of Jelly Roll Morton.

Jelly's Last Jam began previews on Broadway at the Virginia Theatre on March 31, 1992. It opened on April 26. It was produced by Margo Lion and Pamela Koslow-Hines in association with Polygram Diversified Entertainment, 126 Second Avenue Corp./Hal Luftig, Rodger Hess, Jujamcyn Theatres/TV Asahi and Herb Alpert.

George C. Wolfe directed the following cast:

Chimney Man..............................Keith David
Jelly Roll Morton.........................Gregory Hines
The Hunnies ....Mamie Duncan-Gibbs, Stephanie Pope,
                                    Allison M. Williams
The Crowd: Ken Ard, Adrian Bailey, Sherry D. Boone, Brenda
    Braxton, Mary Bond Davis, Ralph Deaton, Melissa Haizlip,
    Cee-Cee Harshaw, Ted L. Levy, Stanley Wayne Mathis, Victoria
    Gabrielle Platt, Gil Pritchett III, Michelle M. Robinson
The People of His Past
    Young Jelly............................Savion Glover
    Sisters ....Victoria Gabrielle Platt, Sherry D. Boone
    Miss Mamie.........................Mary Bond Davis
    Buddy Bolden ....Ruben Santiago-Hudson
    Too-Tight Nora ....Brenda Braxton
    Three-Finger Jake ....Gil Pritchett III
    Gran Mimi ....Ann Duquesnay
    Jack the Bear....................Stanley Wayne Mathis
    Foot-in-Your-Ass Sam ....Ken Ard
    Anita................................Tonya Pinkins
    Melrose Brothers ....Don Johanson, Gordon Joseph Weiss
Ancestors: Adrian Bailey, Mary Bond Davis, Ralph Deaton, Ann
Duquesnay, Melissa Haizlip

Robin Wagner designed the scenery; Jules Fisher, the lighting; Toni-Leslie James, the costumes; Hope Clarke, the choreography; Gregory Hines and Ted L. Levy, the tap choreography; Luther Henderson, the musical supervision and orchestrations; Otts Munderloh, the sound; Barbara Pollitt, mask and puppet design; Jeffrey Frank, hair design; Hughes/Moss & Stanley Soble, casting; Francis A. Hauser, technical supervisor; David Strong Warner, Inc. were the executive producers; Peggy Hill Rosenkranz, Marilyn Hall, Dentsu Inc., the associate producers; Arturo E. Porazzi was the production stage manager; Bernita Robinson and Bonnie L. Becker were the stage managers; Richard Kornberg and Carole Fineman, press representatives.

Jelly's Last Jam was nominated for eleven Tony Awards (including Best Musical, Best Book of a Musical, Best Score and Best Direction of a Musical) and was awarded three (Best Performance by a Leading Actor in a Musical to Gregory Hines; Best Performance by a Featured Actress in a Musical to Tonya Pinkins; and Best Lighting Design).

It was nominated for nine Drama Desk Awards and was awarded six (including Best Book, Best Lyrics, Best Orchestration/Musical Adaptation, Best Lighting, Best Actor in a Musical and Best Featured Actress in a Musical).

The original Broadway cast album was produced by Thomas Z. Shepard for Mercury Records.

A documentary about the creation of *Jelly's Last Jam*, entitled "Jammin' Jelly Roll Morton on Broadway," was produced by Tom Bywaters and Nell Cox for "Great Performances" on PBS-TV. Jac Venza was the executive producer.

JELLY'S
LAST JAM

ACT ONE

PROLOGUE

Lights reveal a large door, carved with Yoruba motifs, floating in the middle of a black void. The stillness is cut by the faint sound of piano riffs, dissonant yet melodic. The door to the void slowly opens and light from within casts the Silhouette of a Man in a top hat and cutaway. Percussive underscore.

The Man slowly enters the void, riding on "a shaft of darkness." It is the Chimney Man—ageless, elegant, otherworldly.

CHIMNEY MAN:
> N' it came to pass that a people were born,
> Then torn from the land that was their home.
> The story of their pain was set forth in music,
> Destined to conquer, take the world by storm.
> N' so messengers were called to spread its glory;
> Go forth Armstrong,
> Go forth Ellington,
> Go forth Basie, Bolden, n' Bechet.

N' it came to pass that a messenger was called
Who came to believe that the message was him.
Yes, he of diamond tooth n' flashy threads;
Yes, he who drinks from the vine of syncopation
But denies the black soil from which
this rhythm was born.

. . . Denies the black soil from which
this rhythm was born!

*On the Chimney Man's signal, there is a blast of music
and the black void begins to magically transform
into. . .*

SCENE I

The Jam

*The Jungle Inn, a run-down club, "somewhere's 'tween
heaven n' hell." Its denizens, hereafter known as the
Crowd—a colorful array of lowdown types—are
"dancin' hard n' gettin' down," as the music continues
to wail.*

*On the Chimney Man's signal, three "creatures"
appear. They are the Hunnies, chorus girls—ethereal and
low. As they begin to "entertain," the Chimney Man
"dissolves" into the black void which still encases the
club.*

HUNNIE ONE: Welcome to the Jungle Inn.
HUNNIE TWO: A lowdown club somewhere's between . . .
HUNNIES: Heaven n' hell.

HUNNIE THREE: Where we jammin'!
CROWD: *Yeah!*
HUNNIE THREE: With Jelly!
CROWD: *Yeah!*
HUNNIES/CROWD: Tonight!

SONG: JELLY'S JAM

HUNNIE ONE:
    TELL YO' MAMA
    AIN'T COMIN' HOME TONIGHT
HUNNIES TWO & THREE:
    WE'RE GONNA JUMP DOWN
    N' JAM WITH JELLY
HUNNIE TWO:
    THE BAND IS BLOWIN'
    THE GIN IS FLOWIN'
HUNNIES ONE & THREE:
    WE GONNA SLUM IT
    N' SLAM WITH JELLY
HUNNIE THREE:
    GIT IT SHAKIN'
    WE GONNA WAIL TONIGHT
HUNNIES ONE & TWO:
    JUMP IN THE BUCKET
    N' JAM WITH JELLY
HUNNIES:
    OOH PAPA
    TIME TO PULL THE STOPPA'
    RAISIN' HELL AT JELLY'S JAM
HUNNIE ONE:
    HO'S N' HIGH-TONES
    HUSTLIN' HONKY TONKS

HUNNIES/CROWD:
> GITTIN' LOWDOWN
> TO JAM WITH JELLY

HUNNIE TWO:
> A LOTTA LOWLIFES
> A LOTTA NO-LIFES

HUNNIES/CROWD:
> GONNA JOIN UP
> N' JAM WITH JELLY

HUNNIE THREE:
> TURN THE HEAT ON
> WE GONNA COOK TONIGHT

HUNNIES/CROWD:
> SO GIT THE JUICE OUT
> N' JAM WITH JELLY

HUNNIES:
> OOH SISTA'
> HOT ENOUGH TO BLISTA'

CROWD:
> RAISIN' HELL AT JELLY'S JAM

> IT'S THE BEST DAMN JAM SINCE WAY BACK
>   WHEN
> IT'S THE ONE LAST CHANCE TO HOWL AGAIN
> IT'S THE "LET'S GIT DRUNK, WHO GIVES A
>   DAMN?"
> LOOK OUT IT'S JELLY'S JAM

> STOMP N' SHOUT
> TURN IT OUT
> PUT YOUR FOOT DOWN DADDY
> HERE I AM
> RAISIN' HELL AT JELLY'S JAM

The Crowd's dancing is raucous and low. The music is blaring and hot. The Hunnies corral the energy of the music and the Crowd as they begin to "conjure up" the spirit of Jelly Roll Morton.

HUNNIES:
C'MON JELLY WE WANT YOUR SOUL
HUNNIES/CROWD:
GONNA JAM JELLY ROLL

WE GITTIN' READY FOR THE ROLL
WE GITTIN' READY FOR THE ROLL
WE GITTIN' READY FOR THE ROLL

AAAAAAHHHH!

The Hunnies and the Crowd continue conjuring up the spirit of Jelly Roll Morton. The dance builds until a slumped figure magically ascends to the stage from below.

HUNNIES/CROWD:
JAZZ ME JELLY ROLL
JAZZ ME JELLY ROLL
JAZZ ME JELLY ROLL
OOOOOOH
JAZZ ME JAZZ ME
JAZZ ME JAZZ ME
JAZZ ME JELLY ROLL
OOOOOOH

The slumped figure enters the club. It's Jelly Roll Morton. As the music and dance continue, Jelly begins to grow in stature until, at the number's end, he is strutting, arrogant and proud.

HUNNIES/CROWD *(Beckoning Jelly):*
COME ON IN!
WHERE YA BEEN?
LET'S GIT DRUNK
WHO GIVES A DAMN?
IT'S PAPA JELLY'S JAM
SWEET PAPA JELLY'S JAM
SMOOTH PAPA JELLY'S JAM
HOT PAPA JELLY
IT'S JELLY'S
JAM!
JAM!
JAM!
Yeah!

The number ends. The Hunnies and the Crowd are busy celebrating Jelly. The Chimney Man appears. On his signal, the action freezes.

CHIMNEY MAN: Well, well, well . . .
WILL YOU LOOK WHO JUST NOW UP N' DIED
COULD IT BE
MISTER JELLY ROLL?

WELCOME JELLY TO THE OTHER SIDE
TIME TO TELL YOUR TALE
N' SAVE YOUR SOUL

IT'S THE NOW OR NEVER,
EVERMORE
END OF THE LINE

N' from this moment on,

YOUR ASS IS MINE

On Chimney Man's signal, the action continues with the Hunnies and the Crowd cheering and hanging on Jelly. Music underscore.

CROWD MEMBER ONE: Jelly, my man, you remember that club just outside of Chicago. *(To the audience)* Y'all remember, that little club.

CROWD MEMBER TWO: The first time I saw "The Roll" was back in . . . er, um, nineteen aught four.

CROWD MEMBER THREE *(A woman; overlapping):* Ooh child I could dance all night to the Chicago Stomp!

CROWD MEMBER FOUR: Remember all them diamonds you had . . .

CROWD MEMBER FIVE: All them suits you had . . .

CROWD MEMBER SIX *(A woman):* All them women you had . . .

CROWD MEMBER SEVEN *(A woman):* You ought to know 'cause he had you twice.

CROWD MEMBER EIGHT: Remember Jelly?

JELLY: Shit yeah, I remember. I remember you . . . n' you. *(To Crowd Member Six)* I don't remember you, but I wish I did. *(To the Crowd)* Maybe a little later she'll remind me.

The Crowd laughs.

JELLY: I remember it all.

SONG: IN MY DAY

JELLY:
I'M TELLIN' YA
IN MY DAY
THIS MAN WAS MADE OF MONEY
YOU KNOW IT, YEAH IN MY DAY

THESE HANDS WERE DRIPPIN' HONEY
I'D FLASH 'EM THAT *SAVOIR FAIRE*
N' TOSS 'EM A SMILE

CROWD MEMBER FOUR: Diamond-studded smile!

JELLY:

WHAT YOU FOLKS CALLED "STYLE"
I USETA CALL THE "HIGH-TONE"
THE "WHOZZAT?"
THE "HOW YOU LEARN TO USE-ZAT!"

IN MY DAY
THIS MAN CAME UP WITH A SOUND
N' INCIDENTALLY IN MY DAY
IT GOT TO GETTIN' AROUND

CROWD *(A trio):*

FROM HIGH-FALUTIN' TO A
HOLE IN THE GROUND

JELLY:

'CAUSE I WAS—
OOH YEAH, GOOD AS THAT!
MISTER MOZART WOULDA
TIPPED HIS HAT
BELIEVE ME WHEN I SAY
I WAS SOMETHIN' IN MY DAY
REALLY SOMETHIN' IN MY DAY

HUNNIES:

THEY CALLED HIM CREOLE BOY
SWEET PAPA JELLY JOY
OOH HOW THAT HARD-LOVIN' DADDY
COULD PLAY
HOT LICKIN' PIANA MAN
COULD ROLL LIKE NO ONE CAN
N' SQUEEZE YOUR LITTLE

TEASE YOUR LITTLE TROUBLES AWAY
OH HOW HIS HANDS WOULD EASE
DOWN THE PIANA KEYS
IT'S LIKE HE WAS STRUTTIN' THE MUSIC
WHENEVER HE'D PLAY

Jelly, "struttin' as if strokin'," dances about, flaunting his prowess and his charm. As Jelly begins to sing again, the Jungle Inn reality begins to fade. Lights reveal Gran Mimi, dressed for mourning and floating in the void, holding a rose and rosary. Jelly is oblivious to her presence.

JELLY:

THEN ONE NIGHT
IT GETS TO FEELIN' TOO STILL
THEN ONE NIGHT
YOU FEEL A SHARP LITTLE CHILL
N' THERE'S THIS—

HUNNIE THREE:

DARKNESS

HUNNIE TWO:

IN THE AIR

HUNNIE ONE:

COMIN' CLOSER
TILL IT'S EVERYWHERE

JELLY:

COMIN' TO STEAL MY STORY
BURY MY NAME, DENY MY GLORY
COMIN' TO BLOW OUT MY LIGHT
TONIGHT!
TONIGHT!

Chimney Man emerges from the void.

CHIMNEY MAN:
TONIGHT!

Music underscore. As Chimney Man speaks, Jelly begins to gasp for air—reliving the sensation of his death.

CHIMNEY MAN: N' in one breath, a man becomes a memory. All he was, what he dreamed, those he loved, lost forever. *Fini.* No more.

On Chimney Man's signal, Jelly recovers. Lights up on the Jungle Inn and the Crowd celebrating Jelly. And floating in the void, Gran Mimi.

CHIMNEY MAN: But if any man's tale deserves to be told, it's The Roll's.

The Crowd commiserates.

JELLY: I couldn't have said it better myself. I don't believe I've had the pleasure.
CHIMNEY MAN: Why I'm him what they call, De Chimney Man. I stand at the corner of Cadaver Avenue and Last Gasp Lane n' sweep folks along the way. Jes' think of me as de doe'man. Or *le concierge* to your soul.
JELLY: I like that.
CHIMNEY MAN: I figured you would.
JELLY: *Le concierge* to my soul. So Chim . . . *(Confidentially)* . . . does this mean that I'm already . . . ?
CHIMNEY MAN: Terminally inclined? Afraid so. Which is why there's not a moment to lose. There are so many tales—
JELLY: Left untold.
CHIMNEY MAN: So many truths—
JELLY: Locked inside of lies.
CHIMNEY MAN: But tonight is your night Jelly.
JELLY: My night!

CHIMNEY MAN: To relive n' recreate that which was.

CHIMNEY MAN: N' in a flash, that
which you remember, becomes
real. N' the Crowd, this club,
this audience, this night, the
veiled lady who stands so
stunningly reposed, are here to
serve only you. Ah yes,
tonight we gonna jam Jelly!

CROWD (Whispered):
JAZZ ME
JELLY ROLL
JAZZ ME
JELLY ROLL
JAZZ ME
JELLY ROLL
(Etc.)

JELLY: You mean Jam wit' Jelly.
CHIMNEY MAN: But of course.

Music up.

CROWD:
JAM!
JELLY:
MOVE OVER, HERE I AM!
CROWD:
JAM!
CHIMNEY MAN:
GIT READY! TIME TO JAM!
CROWD:
JAM!
JELLY/CHIMNEY MAN:
THE STORY OF THE ROLL
CHIMNEY MAN:
HIS HEART
JELLY:
HIS SONG
CHIMNEY MAN:
HIS SOUL

JELLY/CHIMNEY MAN/HUNNIES/CROWD:
　IT'S JELLY'S . . .
　JAM!
　JAM!
　JAM!

As the music blares, the Crowd and the Jungle Inn disappear into the void. Jelly and Chimney Man look on as the Hunnies take center stage.

SCENE 2

In the Beginning

HUNNIE THREE: Introducing . . .
HUNNIE ONE: The blueprint for perfection . . .
HUNNIE TWO: Ferdinand Le Menthe Morton!

Jelly is joined by Young Jelly, early teens. He is as rakishly charming as his older self.

YOUNG JELLY: Also known as . . . Young Jelly.
JELLY: Same classic profile.
YOUNG JELLY: Same regal brow.
JELLY *(Indicating Young Jelly)*: It's hard to believe someone who looks this good . . .
YOUNG JELLY *(Indicating Jelly)*: Could get even better, but . . .
JELLY/YOUNG JELLY: What can we say.
JELLY: 'Course now "The Roll" wasn't always so in control. For you see I . . .
YOUNG JELLY: Me . . .
JELLY: We . . . are the progeny of one of the oldest—

YOUNG JELLY: —and most genteel Creole families in New Orleans.

Lights reveal a turn-of-the-century New Orleans parlor, replete with five "ancestors" holding frames to simulate portraits of Creole Ancestors. Two young Creole girls, Amede and Viola, stand perfectly posed holding white fans.

JELLY: Classically trained by the finest musicians of the day, while those of darker hues lived in shacks n' crooned the blues, I would sit in the parlor, under the watchful gaze of my Creole ancestors . . .
YOUNG JELLY: And I would play the piano . . .
JELLY: As my two beautiful sisters, Amede and Viola, would sing . . . and dance . . .

As Young Jelly "plays," Amede and Viola dance and the Ancestors sing.

SONG: THE CREOLE WAY

AMEDE/VIOLA:
    LA LA LA LA
    LA LA LA LA
ANCESTORS:
    OUR SKIN IS FAIR
    OUR BLOOD EUROPEAN
    OUR WAVY HAIR
    SOMEWHERE IN BETWEE-EN
    NOT A GRIT OR COLLARD GREEN
    COME WHAT MAY
AMEDE/VIOLA:
    LA LA LA LA LA LA
ANCESTOR ONE:
    DON'T YOU AGREE?

ANCESTOR TWO:
  OF COURSE
ANCESTORS THREE & FIVE:
  MAIS OUI
AMEDE/VIOLA:
  LA LA LA LA
ANCESTORS:
  THAT'S THE CREOLE WAY

ANCESTOR FOUR:	AMEDE/VIOLA:
WHILE OTHERS WILL DEBAUCH THEMSELVES NIGHTLY	LA LA LA LA

ANCESTOR TWO:

WE DANCE QUADRILLES AND MINGLE POLITELY	LA LA LA LA

ANCESTORS/AMEDE/VIOLA:
  TO A TUNE THAT'S
  BRILLIANTLY LIGHT
  AND GAY!

YOUNG JELLY:	ANCESTORS/AMEDE/VIOLA:
ALL I DO IS PLAY AND PLAY	LA LA LA LA
PLAY WHAT I PLAYED YESTERDAY	LA LA LA LA LA LA
SAME OLD LA LA LA	LA LA LA LA
IN THE SAME OLD KEY	LA LA LA LA
WHAT IF I COULD VARY THAT	
CHANGE A RHYTHM, ADD A FLAT	
UNTIL IT FEELS MORE LIKE ME?	

The Ancestors abruptly stop singing.

ANCESTORS/AMEDE/VIOLA: Like you! *(Cornering Young Jelly)*
ANCESTOR ONE:
>You're given notes
>And so you will play them

ANCESTORS THREE & FOUR:
>You're given rules
>And you will obey them

ANCESTORS:
>GOOD BOYS LEARN TO FOLLOW
>FOOLS DECIDE TO STRAY
>WHICH SHALL IT BE?
>WHICH SHALL IT BE?
>ANSWER US BOY!

YOUNG JELLY *(Deafeated)*:
>THE CREOLE WAY

ANCESTORS/AMEDE/VIOLA:
>THE CREOLE WAY

Lights out on the Ancestors, Amede and Viola. As Jelly crosses to console Young Jelly, the Parlor fades away.

SONG: THE WHOLE WORLD'S WAITIN' TO SING YOUR SONG

JELLY *(Scatting)*:
>WAH-WAH-WAH-WAH
>WAH-WAH-WAH-WAH-WAH-WAH
>THAT AIN'T YOU
>NOT THE "YOU" YOU GONNA BE
>THE MAN YOU WANNA BE IS ME
>YEAH YEAH YEAH

YOUNG JELLY:
> YEAH, YEAH . . . NO

JELLY:
> READY OR NOT, BOY
> GONNA BE HOT, BOY
> THE WHOLE WORLD'S WAITIN'
> TO SING YOUR SONG!
> I TELL YA
>
> YOU WANT A NEW
> A "NEVER-BEFORE" SOUND
> I'LL TAKE YOU TO
> A "SOON-TO-BE-YOUR" SOUND
> THE WHOLE WORLD'S WAITIN'
> TO SING YOUR SONG

YOUNG JELLY: But they just said . . .

JELLY:
> FORGET WHAT THEY TOLD YOU
> C'MON AHEAD
> AIN'T NUTHIN' TO HOLD YOU
> THE WHOLE WORLD'S WAITIN' TO SING YOUR
> > SONG
>
> YOU'LL BE
> MISTER "KEEP-'EM-COMIN'"
> KING OF THE GOOD-TIME RAG
> FAST LICKS
> FANCY SYNCOPATION

JELLY/YOUNG JELLY:
> N' ALL KINDS OF REASON TO BRAG!

JELLY:	YOUNG JELLY:
YOU ARE THE ONE	. . . THE ONE
THE SUN'S GONNA RISE ON	. . . GONNA
THE ONE THE WORLD	RISE ON
IS KEEPIN' ITS EYES ON	
THE WHOLE WORLD'S WAITIN'	
TO SING . . .	

*Jelly illustrates a riff of syncopation—i.e., tap or scat—
as lights reveal stylized fragments of the French Quarter
and the People of the Street. Their patchwork attire,
colorful wares and percussive street cries envelop the
stage.*

BEIGNET MAN: Fresh hot beignets!

JELLY: There's a whole other world beyond these parlor
walls.

RAG MAN: Get your rags, man!

JELLY: A symphony of sound to be orchestrated . . .

GATOR MAN: Snake oil!

TIN-A-FEEX MAN: Fix yuh tin!

JELLY: Syncopated . . .

GUMBO LADY: Gumbo filé ya-ya!

JELLY: N' they're all waiting on you.

YARD GIRLS *(The Hunnies):*

WAH-OOH WAH-OOH WAH-OOH

JELLY: Yard girls everywhere.

YARD GIRLS:

DO DADDY DO
DO DADDY DO
DO DADDY DO DA

JELLY: Spasm band . . .

*A Spasm Band—black boys in tattered clothes—plays
washboards, pots and pans.*

JELLY: Here comes the beignet man!
BEIGNET MAN:
FRESH HOT BEIGNETS!
FRESH HOT BEIGNETS!
BEIG-NETS!
JELLY: The lady with the gumbo pan . . .
GUMBO LADY:
GIT IT WHILE IT'S HOTTA
HOTTA-HOTTA
GIT IT WHILE IT'S HOTTA
JELLY: The brick-dust lady . . .
BRICK-DUST LADY:
ZOZO LA BRIQUE
JELLY: Tin-a-Feex and Gator Man . . .
TIN-A-FEEX MAN:
TIN TIN TIN-A-FEEX
FIX YUH TIN
GATOR MAN:
I GOT YUH SNAKE OIL
JELLY: Root man, Ragman, Green Sass Man . . .
RAGMAN:
GIT YOUR RAGS-AH READY
FO' DE OLE RAGMAN
GREEN SASS MAN:
CANTAL-OPE-AH
FROM DE GREEN SASS MAN
ROOT MAN:
ROOTS! ROOTS!
ROOTS FOR LOVIN'

ROOTS FOR LIVIN'
ROOT MAN

The People of the Street abruptly freeze.

JELLY: The whole world's waitin' . . . *make your song . . .*

*Young Jelly stands motionless, overwhelmed by his task.
He then begins to conduct, adding rhythm on top of
rhythm.*

YARD GIRLS:

DO DADDY DO
DO DADDY DO
DO DADDY DO DA
OH-WAH-OOH
WAH-OH WAH-OH

SPASM BAND: *(Rhythms—four bars)*

BEIGNET MAN:

COME BUY-O BEIGNET MAN

GUMBO LADY:

LADY WITH THE GUMBO PAN . . .
GET IT WHILE IT'S HOTTA, HOTTA, HOTTA

BRICK-DUST LADY:

ZOZO LA BRIQUE

TIN-A-FEEX MAN:

TIN TIN TIN-A-FEEX
FIX YUH TIN

GATOR MAN:

I GOT YUH SNAKE OIL

GREEN SASS MAN:

CANTAL-OPE-AH

RAGMAN:

GET YUH RAGS AH READY
FOR DE RAGMAN . . .

ROOT MAN:
> ROOTS! ROOTS!
> ROOTS FOR LOVIN'
> ROOTS FOR LIVIN' *(Etc.)*

Jelly steps in. He dances/scats a percussive rhythm. Young Jelly repeats it. Jelly creates another rhythm. Young Jelly repeats it. The call and response grows and grows until Jelly and Young Jelly are dancing/scatting as if one.

PEOPLE OF THE STREET:
> YOU! YOU! YOU! YOU!
> YOU! YOU! YOU! YOU!

> YOU'RE THE ONE
> THE SUN'S GONNA RISE ON
> THE ONE WE'RE KEEPIN' OUR EYES ON
> JUST WAITIN' TO SING YOUR SONG
> YEAH! YEAH! YEAH!

> SLIDE THAT SOUND
> ROLL THAT RHYTHM
> SYNCOPATE THE STREET-BEAT WITH 'EM
> THE WHOLE WORLD, THE WHOLE WORLD
> IS WAITING TO SING YOUR . . .

Final tap break.

PEOPLE OF THE STREET:
> . . . YOUR SONG.

The street fades away as Jelly and Young Jelly applaud/toast one another. The Chimney Man and the Hunnies appear. Lights out on Young Jelly.

CHIMNEY MAN: Bravo Jelly, bravo. But how did your ancestors feel about you cavorting with *un gens du commun*. They couldn't have been too pleased.

The Hunnies hold up a picture frame as Chimney Man "becomes" a Creole Ancestor.

CHIMNEY MAN:
FERDINAND!

JELLY *(Amused)*: You? One of my ancestors?

CHIMNEY MAN *(Aside)*: Some folks like a bit of cream in their coffee. Just think of me as the coffee in your family's cream. *(As Ancestor; recitative)*

HOW MANY TIMES DO WE HAVE TO TELL YOU
WE ARE WHO WE ARE
N' WE ARE NOT WHO WE ARE NOT!
BEATING ON POTS NEVER HAS BEEN
AND NEVER WILL BE MUSIC
MUSIC IS THE FRENCH OPERA HOUSE

Music underscore.

CHIMNEY MAN: Ah yes, the French Opera House, that bastion of culture n' grace, where the lilting melodies of Massenet warmed the hearts of all Creoles. But not the soul of Creole boy. Jelly, you forgot to tell them that when you was just a lad, yo' daddy run off n' yo' mama up n' died.

JELLY: Wait a minute. Wait a—

CHIMNEY MAN *(Overlapping)*: N' when you got a case of them lonely boy blues, Massenet is simply not enough.

On the Chimney Man's signal, lights reveal Miss Mamie.

JELLY: . . . this is my life n' I'm gonna tell it my way.

MAMIE: *(Overlapping):* Oooh child, I'd know that behind of yours a mile away.

JELLY: Mamie!

They embrace.

MAMIE: Little Sweet Butt!

JELLY *(Nuzzling Mamie's cleavage):* Big Mamie.

MAMIE: Git yo' head outta there, boy!

JELLY *(To audience):* Everybody, I'd like y'all to meet the melodic, the magnificent, the mellifluous Miss Mamie—known 'round N'awlins as the Blues Queen of Rampart Street n' Perdito.

MAMIE *(Asking the audience):* Y'all ever hear of me? *(Pause for audience response . . .)* I said, d'yall ever hear of me? *(Once the audience responds . . .)* Folks'll lie as soon as lookin' at you. *(Laughs)* Darlin', don't feel bad. My story lasted 'bout as long as my song. *(To Jelly)* Not like some folks who done gone off n' got famous. Aww but in my day, from the tip of my titties to the bottom of my shoes . . .

I DRANK, DRUNK, FEEL, FUNK, FELT ME SOME BLUES

N' these ain't no pretend titties, so you know my shit wuz strong. N' there wuzn't but one man who could do the blues the way the blues ought to be done!

JELLY *(Modestly):* Well now, Mamie, I've never considered the blues my forte, however . . .

MAMIE: Sweet Butt, ain't nobody tawkin' 'bout you. Now when it comes to strokin', you the one. But when it comes to smokin' you know there was none other than—

JELLY/MAMIE: Buddy Bolden!

Lights reveal Buddy Bolden playing his cornet.

MAMIE: The man hit notes only colored folks n' heaven could hear.

JELLY: I remember the first time I went sneakin' off n' met King Buddy.

Lights reveal Young Jelly cautiously walking down a series of alleyways and streets depicted by doorframes.

JELLY: I musta been 'bout thirteen at the time. It was just past near dark, n' I was out walkin' where good Creoles didn't go, when I heard this

SOULFULLY, WOEFULLY, LOWDOWN SOUND . . .

Buddy plays a riff.

HUNNIE TWO:
FOLLOW THAT UPTOWN-RAGTIME-TAG-ALONG

Young Jelly walks down an alley full of Crib Girls— uptown prostitutes.

HUNNIE THREE:
FOLLOW THAT UPTOWN-RAGTIME-TAG-ALONG

Young Jelly walks down a street where a couple is grinding, and gets caught in the middle of Two Men fighting. Buddy Bolden plays.

HUNNIE ONE:
FOLLOW THAT UPTOWN-RAGTIME-TAG-ALONG
HUNNIES:
BARRELHOUSE BLUES.

Young Jelly comes to a doorway. As he walks through it, lights reveal . . .

SCENE 3

Goin' Uptown

Buddy Bolden takes command of the club stage. He is joined by a Piano Player and Miss Mamie. The Jungle Inn Crowd becomes Buddy's Uptown Crowd as they gather in a circle on chairs around Buddy and Miss Mamie.

SONG: MICHIGAN WATER

MISS MAMIE:
> MICHIGAN WATER
> TASTE LIKE SHERRY WINE
> MEAN SHERRY WINE
> MICHIGAN WATER
> TASTE LIKE SHERRY WINE
> MISSISSIPPI WATER
> TASTE LIKE TURPENTINE

BUDDY:
> RAMPART STREET GAL
> SHE GOT A BLACK CAT BONE

MISS MAMIE:
> A BLACK CAT BONE

BUDDY:
> OH RAMPART STREET GAL
> SHE GOT A BLACK CAT BONE

MISS MAMIE:
> A BLACK CAT BONE

BUDDY:
> THE HO' DID HER HOODOO
> N' NOW I CAN'T LEAVE HER ALONE

Music underscore.

BUDDY: *(To audience):* How many y'all ever loved yo'selves a brownskin gal?

The Crowd responds.

BUDDY: Oooowee, wuzn't it sweet.

The Crowd responds.

BUDDY: Ya git to understand why God made the earth like he did. All rich n' dark. Jes' makes ya wanna plow all night long.

I loved me a brownskin gal. N' thought she loved me till one day she got up, put on her Sunday-go-to-meetin'-dress, n' some waves in her head, n' went downtown. Said she wanted to git herself a high-tone man.

I said, "Now babee, did ya git hit in the head doin' Miss Ann's laundry or what? They don't want you downtown, 'cauz jes' like yo' ass, yo' face is brown. What you be wantin' after some Creole priss, wit' his nose all up in the air. He may know the right way to hold a fork. But a good fork ain't nuthin' compared to a good . . .

Buddy makes his cornet "growl." The Crowd responds.

BUDDY: All them Creoles is good for is . . .

Buddy sees Young Jelly standing around, "feeling" the music.

BUDDY: Well now, what have's we here? Say Frenchy, yo' Mama know you hangin' out with us darktown folk?

The Crowd taunts Young Jelly.

27

YOUNG JELLY: My name's not Frenchy! It's Ferdinand Le Menthe Morton!

BUDDY: Sure as shit sounds like Frenchy to me. Ya look like ya got music in ya. Whatcha play?

YOUNG JELLY: Everything.

BUDDY: Do tell?

YOUNG JELLY: Piano, guitar, mandolin . . .

BUDDY: We fresh outta mandolins, how 'bout "throwin' a roll"?

YOUNG JELLY: Huh?

BUDDY: The piano!

The Piano Player steps aside and lets Young Jelly take his place.

BUDDY: Ya know "Lonesome Bed Blues"?

Young Jelly shakes his head "no."

BUDDY: "Conti Street Blues"?

Young Jelly shakes his head "no."

BUDDY: "Creole-Boy-Don't-Know-Shit Blues?"

YOUNG JELLY: I know "The Miserere" from *Il Trovatore.*

BUDDY: That ain't no music; the notes is written out, tellin' ya what's gon' come next. That's like wakin' up in the mornin' n' knowin' you gonna be alive at the end of the day. That may be the way you Creoles live, but it is not the way we do things uptown!

The Crowd commiserates.

BUDDY: Frenchy, meet Too-Tight Nora n' Three-Finger Jake.

Nora and Jake, two rough types, join Buddy.

BUDDY: Jake, show 'em that walk you do called "Shootin' the Agaite."

Jake "walks." Buddy, Young Jelly and the Uptown Crowd cheer him on.

BUDDY: Nora baby, strut that strut that gits the sun so hot, it's got to go home for the night n' cool off.

Nora "struts." Buddy, Young Jelly and the Crowd go wild.

MISS MAMIE:
NOW WHEN YOU PLAYIN'
WHAT THEY WALKIN'
THAT'S MUSIC!

(Spoken; to Young Jelly) Go on Sweet Butt, n' play that piano!

Buddy and Young Jelly play; the Crowd dances.

MISS MAMIE:
I'M GONNA WEAR OSTRICH PLUMES N' SATIN
A HORSEHAIR WIG THREE FEET HIGH
SO ALL YOU GUMBO-EATIN' BITCHES
CAN KISS MY ASS GOODBYE
MISSISSIPPI WATER AIN'T NO FRIEND OF MINE
MICHIGAN WATER TASTE LIKE SHERRY WINE
WE SAY
MISSISSIPPI WATER TASTE LIKE TURPENTINE

The number ends.

MAMIE: Ferdinand took to sneakin' off n' hangin' with Buddy n' that uptown, lowdown Crowd.

JELLY: Tradin' swaggers n' swills n' thrillin' the Crowd . . .

YOUNG JELLY: . . . with my high-brow know-how!

JELLY: N' it was 'round about now that I invented jazz.

*On the Chimney Man's signal, Jelly and the Crowd
freeze.*

CHIMNEY MAN:
> And it came to pass that a messenger was called
> Who came to believe that the message was him . . .

*On a second signal, Chimney Man "unfreezes" Jelly and
the Crowd and the action continues. As Young Jelly
plays the piano, the Uptown Crowd, Buddy, Mamie,
Jelly, and the Hunnies as Storyville Whores celebrate
and embrace Young Jelly and his music.*

SONG: SHORT PIANO ROLL

UPTOWN CROWD:
> SWEET AS JELLY ON A ROLL
> SWEET JELLY ON A ROLL
> GO ON JELLY N' PLAY THAT ROLL
> THAT'S WHY THEY CALL HIM MISTER
> THAT'S WHY THEY CALL HIM MISTER
> THAT'S WHY THEY CALL HIM MISTER
> JELLY ROLL
> ROLL . . .
> ROLL . . .
> ROLL . . .

*During the above, the uptown world begins to fade into
the void. Jelly and Young Jelly find themselves enveloped
in the shadow of a Veiled Woman standing in front of a
New Orleans door.*

CHIMNEY MAN: *Je me presente . . . Madame Mimi Pachet . . .*

The Veiled Woman lifts her veil. It's Gran Mimi, matronly, elegant, severe.

GRAN MIMI: *Vini citi!* I said come here.

Young Jelly runs to her.

CHIMNEY MAN: Wrought iron draped in lace n' brocade.

GRAN MIMI: How many times do I have to tell you, we are who we are and we are not who we are not.

YOUNG JELLY: But I was only—

GRAN MIMI: Silence!

CHIMNEY MAN: What Jelly left out of his revisionist reverie, is *la vérité* . . . *(Aside)* . . . that's French for "the boy be tellin' lies." For you see, after his mama was no more, he n' his sisters were raised by Gran Mimi. *N'est pas,* Jelly?

JELLY *(Nonchalant):* This never happened.

CHIMNEY MAN: N' once she found out 'bout you jammin' wit' them niggas n' messin' wit' them whores—

GRAN MIMI: You are not fit to be Creole. You are no grandchild of mine.

YOUNG JELLY: If you'd only let me—

GRAN MIMI: I said silence!

JELLY *(With growing intensity):* This never happened.

CHIMNEY MAN *(Overlapping):* Shall I tell 'em what came next or shall you—

JELLY *(Emphatic):* I said this never happened!

CHIMNEY MAN: I'd be delighted! Ole Mimi got so beside herself, she jes' hauled off n' . . .

Gran Mimi slaps Young Jelly. Music underscore.

CHIMNEY MAN: In case y'all didn't git that, she just hauled off n'—

31

Gran Mimi slaps again. This time Jelly responds as if he's been hit. Young Jelly falls and cowers on the ground.

SONG: THE BANISHMENT

GRAN MIMI:
GET AWAY, BOY
WANT YOU AWAY FROM MY DOOR
GET AWAY, BOY
WANT YOU AWAY FROM MY DOOR

I KNOW YOU BEEN STAYING OUT
EVERY NIGHT
KNOW YOU BEEN SNEAKING HOME
'FORE IT'S LIGHT

COME BACK HERE SMELLING OF ALL
THAT'S LOW
OF THINGS I DON'T WANT TO KNOW
OOOOOHHHHHHH

IF YOU SPIT IN THE WATER
THERE'S NO GOING BACK TO THE WELL

You shame the name of *la famille* . . .

SPIT IN THE WATER
OH, THERE'S NO GOING BACK TO THE WELL

You shame the memory of your mother . . .

YOU LAY DOWN WITH DIRT
YOU GONNA CARRY THAT SMELL

(Scats)

OOOH
WOH
OH
WOH-WOH-WOH-WOH
OOOOH
OH-WOH-WOH-OH-WOH

TU N'EST PAS CREOLE
YOU ARE NOT CREOLE!
YOU BEEN LAYING WITH DIRT
YOU ARE NOT CREOLE!
THAT'S WHY I'M TELLING YOU
YOU HAVE NO FAMILY—NOW GO!

YOUNG JELLY:
    PLEASE!
GRAN MIMI:
    GO!
YOUNG JELLY:
    PLEASE!
GRAN MIMI:
    VA!
    VA!
    VA!

Jelly crosses in to console his younger self.

JELLY:
    LONELY BOY, HE
    HURTIN' SO BAD INSIDE
    LOST WHATEVER KIND OF
    LOVIN' HE'S KNOWN
    LONELY BOY,

HURTIN' SO BAD INSIDE
FROM NOW ON
GONNA FEEL SO ALONE
ALONE
ALONE

GRAN MIMI:

GET AWAY FROM MY DOOR

Gran Mimi and her door fade. Young Jelly fades into
the void. The number ends. The Chimney Man crosses
to Jelly.

JELLY: You shouldn't have done that.

CHIMNEY MAN: I know, I know. It's your life, and you want
to tell it your way. But in telling the story of Jelly, the
story of jazz, ya gotta have grit to go with the gravy—ya
gotta have pain, to go with the song.

JELLY: Listen Shine, why don't you just go stand over in the
dark somewhere, n' leave the light on me.

CHIMNEY MAN: N' because you said so I'm supposed to go?
Because your Creole ass commanded, I'm supposed to
obey? I hate to disappoint you Jelly, but I'm up n' in yo'
shit n' I'm gonna stay there till I break you.

JELLY: Aww he'p me he'p me Shine 'cause I do's be scared.

CHIMNEY MAN: You have no idea—

JELLY: No, you're the one who has no idea. All my life I
been fightin' to git what should have been given n' I'll
be damned if I'm gonna let you or anybody else tell me
a damn thing about my life or the way I lived it. I know
what I deserve n' I'm gonna—

CHIMNEY MAN: What you deserve? What you deserve is for
me to sweep your arrogant ass straight to hell.

JELLY: Well, why don't you "Kiss my arrogant Creole ass."

Music underscore.

CHIMNEY MAN: I take that back. Hell's too good for you.
Ever hear of East St. Louis? Piss me off again n' you
gonna be giggin' in ole West Hell. Even the devil doesn't
go there after dark.

JELLY: Out my way, Shine, I'm gittin' mine tonight.

CHIMNEY MAN: To relive your past with none of the pain is a
lie. N' for every tale you lace with a lie, I'm gonna be
there.

JELLY: N' so will I, Shine. Go on n' try, Shine.

CHIMNEY MAN: I'm gonna drag you through it.

JELLY: Alright Shine, let's do it!

*Just as Jelly turns, Chimney Man "vanishes" and Jelly
finds standing before him Jack the Bear—dark-skinned,
and with an easy-going Southern charm. Music
underscore continues.*

SCENE 4

The Journey to Chicago

JELLY (Overjoyed): Jack!

JACK: Jelly . . . my partner!

JELLY: My man!

JACK: My "I cover your back."

JELLY: N' you cover mine.

JELLY/JACK: Brothers to the end!

They laugh and embrace.

JELLY: Everybody, meet my ace-boon-coon, Jack the Bear!

JACK: How y'all doin?

JELLY: Jack n' I first met ridin' the rails to anywhere's other than where we was from. Jack, tell 'em where ya got ya name.

JACK *(Embarrassed)*: Jelly man, they don't wanna hear 'bout how—

JELLY: He stole it. Ha! Took it from this Mississippi gangster n' claimed it as his own.

JACK: Hell, his ass wuz dead. Lotta good it was gonna do him. 'Sides, I like the way it fit me. "Jack . . . the Bear."

JELLY: Tell 'em what your real name is.

JACK: Awww man . . .

JELLY: His mama named him Clovis. Ha! *(Laughs)* Clovis n' Ferd. Two of the sorriest lookin' fools you'd ever wanna see. Me with my high wata' pants n' oversized suit.

JACK: My hat too big n' these hand-me-down shoes. Good thing we never walked 'cross no mirror. Otherwise I'd ah gone runnin' back to 'Bama n' you to New Orleans.

JELLY: Jack my man, ya don't understand. The world's gonna be our home. Lotsa money's gon' be our home. Too many women . . .

Music out.

JELLY: . . . that'll be my home. But I'll let you come visit.

Hunnies bring on "hick" jackets and hats for Jack and Jelly. A cattle car appears. During the whole "Somethin' More" sequence, the cattle car transforms into various locales; i.e., a Pool Hall, a Dance Hall, etc.

SONG: SOMETHIN' MORE

JACK:

GOT NO LUNCH

JELLY:

WE GOT NO DINNER

JACK:

POCKETS THIN

JELLY:

N' GITTIN' THINNER

JACK:

GOT NO BED
'CEPT THE FLOOR

JELLY:

NO, THAT AIN'T IT
THERE'S SOMETHIN' MORE

HENRY FORD,
HE'S GITTIN' RICHER
WHY NOT US?
YA GET THE "PITCHER?"

JACK:

WELL, WHAT THE HELL
WE WAITIN' FOR

JELLY, JACK:

SO LET US GIT US SOMETHIN' MORE!

JELLY:

LOTSA SUITS—THE HANDMADE KIND
WEAR SIX A DAY IF I'VE A MIND

JACK:

SHOES THAT FIT—LIVIN' FAT
N' A BIG WIDE COMFORTABLE BED

JELLY:

BRAND NEW TOWNS
NEW WAY OF TALKIN'

JACK:
   RIDE THE RAILS
   INSTEAD OF WALKIN'
JELLY/JACK:
   FORGET THE OLD US
   OUT-IN-THE-COLD US
   FORGET WHAT WE AIN'T HAD BEFORE
   TIME TO HUSTLE US
   SOMETHIN' MORE!
   SOMETHIN' MORE!
   SOMETHIN' . . .

Jelly and Jack find themselves inside a Pool Hall. The lights are dim and the Men dangerous. The Hunnies appear as Low Girls. A Bouncer hands Jelly a pool cue, bets are placed and the game begins.

The Pool Game

An oily Pool Player takes his first shot.

HUNNIES *(Chanting seductively):*
   Nine ball—*unnh!*
   In the pocket!

The Player takes another shot.

HUNNIES:
   Ten ball—*unnh!*
   In the pocket!

The Player takes another shot.

HUNNIES:
   You—*unnh!*
   Missed the pocket! Next!

Jelly takes his first shot.

JELLY: I'm gonna hit that one. N' that one's gonna hit that one. N' they both gonna go in. I hope.

HUNNIES:
> Seven, five—*unnh! unnh!*
> In the pocket!

Jelly takes his next shot.

HUNNIES:
> Four, three—*unnh! unnh!*
> In the pocket!

As Jelly prepares to take his next shot . . .

HUNNIES:
> Eight ball
> Take it home now . . .
> Take it home now . . .
> Take it home now . . .

They all watch the ball slowly roll in.

HUNNIES:
> *Unnh!*

As Jelly goes to retrieve his winnings, lights out on the Hunnies. The Pool Player covers the money with his foot. Jelly feigns surrender. He and Jack turn to go. The Pool Player and his Men begin to laugh. Their laughter is cut short when Jelly turns back and hits the Player with his cue. On the hit, lights out on pool scene and up on Chimney and the Hunnies. Percussive underscore.

CHIMNEY MAN:
SINCE GRANDMA KICKED HIM OUT THE DO'

HUNNIES:
> HE WANTS SOMETHIN' MO'
> HE WANTS SOMETHIN' MO'

CHIMNEY MAN:
> DON'T PLAY HIS MUSIC LIKE HE DID BEFO'

HUNNIES:
> HE WANTS SOMETHIN' MO'
> HE WANTS SOMETHIN' MO'

CHIMNEY MAN:
> GOT AN EMPTY SPACE
> INSIDE OF HIM
> N' HE'S OUT TO FILL IT
> TO THE BRIM
> WITH A HANDOUT

HUNNIE THREE:
> A HUSTLE

HUNNIE ONE:
> A FIVE-DOLLAR HO'

HUNNIE TWO:
> FROM A CINCINNATI CATHOUSE

HUNNIE THREE:
> TO A DIVE IN MONROE

CHIMNEY MAN:
> CREOLE BOY WANTS

CHIMNEY MAN/HUNNIES/CROWD:
> MO' MO' MO' MO'
> MO' MO' MO' MO'

A Bordello

Lights reveal Jack caught up in a card game and Jelly surrounded by Women.

HUNNIES:
> IN A SPORTIN' HOUSE DOWN NATCHEZ WAY
> JACK N' JELLY STOP TO PLAY

JELLY:
> JACK PULLS OFF A POKER PLOY

CROWD *(At card table; amazed):*
> OOOOH!

JACK:
> WHILE JELLY'S INSIDE SPREADIN' JOY

WOMEN *(Orgasmically):*
> AAAAAH!

Jelly and Jack dance/strut to the next locale.

A Chain Gang

HUNNIES:
> IN MOBILE
> WE DO MEAN 'BAMA
> ALMOST SWUNG A CHAIN-GANG HAMMA

CHAIN-GANG MEN:
> UNNH!
> UNNH!

JACK:
> JUDGE SAID "FO' YEARS"

JELLY:
> WE SAID "NO YEARS—
> SO LONG 'BAMA—"

JACK:
> "GOTTA SCRAM-A!"

Jelly and Jack "escape."

HUNNIES/CROWD:
> OOH YEAH! OOH YEAH!
> BA-DA-BA-DA-BA-DA-BA-DA-BA-DA

HUNNIES:
> LEFT KENTUCKY
> FEELIN' LUCKY
> TURNIN' NASHVILLE
> INTO CASH-VILLE
> SITTIN' PRETTY IN
> YAZOO CITY
> PUT SOME JUICE IN
> TUSCALOOS—

Jelly and Jack reappear in dapper attire.

JELLY/JACK:
> EVERY DAY
> ALONG THE WAY

JELLY:
> GITTIN' SMARTER

JACK:
> GITTIN' QUICKER

JELLY:
> SMOOTHER

JACK:
> BETTER

JELLY/JACK:
> SHARPER
> SLICKER
>
> GOOD TIMES KNOCKIN'
> AT OUR DOOR—

*As Jelly and Jack traverse the countryside, men strut
past them announcing the shifting locales—"Entering
Memphis"; "70 Miles to Biloxi"; "Cincinnati Population
451,160"; "Brownsville, Southernmost Town in USA".*

HUNNIES:

SOMETHIN' MORE
SOMETHIN' MORE
SOMETHIN' MORE
SOMETHIN' MORE
SOMETHIN' MORE
SOMETHIN' MORE
SOMETHIN' MORE
SOMETHIN' MORE

The Hunnies envelop Jelly and sing seductively.

HUNNIES:

CHICAGO—THAT'S WHERE THE MONEY'S FLYIN'
CHICAGO—THAT'S WHERE THE MUSIC'S
    SWINGIN'
CHICAGO
CHICAGO
CHICAGO
YEAH!

JELLY *(To Jack):* Jack pack yo' bags n' a new attitude. We headin' for Chi-ca-go!

JACK: Jelly my man, I'm all for somethin' more, as long as it ain't too much. Now, a cousin of mine, he went to this Chicago place, n' was never heard from again.

JELLY: That's 'cause it's hard to write home when ya got a woman in your left hand n' a wad of money in your right. Jes' look at us. We too pretty to touch, n' too

smart to lose. Chicago is our kinda town. I hear they
got buildings as high as the Tower of Babel; trains
that fly like Ezekiel's wheel; n' women . . . like Bathsheba . . .

JACK: Good God!

JELLY: Who love to be touched . . . in all the wrong places.

Music underscore out.

JACK: Jelly?

JELLY: Yeah Jack?

JACK: What say we go git us—

Music up.

JELLY:

SOMETHIN' MORE—

JACK:

WE TALKIN' WOMEN

JELLY:

SOMETHIN' MORE—

JACK:

STARK NAKED WOMEN

JELLY:

SOMETHIN' MORE—

JACK:

YES LORD, BATHSHEBA

JELLY:

SOMETHIN' . . .

JACK:

WAITIN' . . .

JELLY:

SOMETHIN' . . .

JACK:
> WANTIN'. . . . .

JELLY/JACK:
> MORE

The Dance Hall

Jelly and Jack turn to find themselves in a run-down Dance Hall. A mediocre Piano Player is pounding out a tune as Couples half-heartedly dance.

JACK: This dive ain't Chicago! Where's Bathsheba?

JELLY: Before we hit big time, I gotta make sure I've still got the touch.

JACK: But this ain't no pool hall, it's a dance hall.

JELLY: These hands can do more than jes' curl their way 'round a cue. *(Loud-talking)* Jack my man, I thought you told me this was a hot juke joint. Sheeet! Nuthin' but cheap liquor, beat chicks n' bad music.

The Piano Player stops playing, couples stop dancing. Jelly continues to loud-talk, oblivious to the shift in attitude.

JELLY *(Laughing)*: We tawkin' three strikes n' yo' ass is out.

WAITRESS *(Threatening; to Jack)*: Whut he say?

JACK: Ha-ha-ha. He was just mumblin' 'bout what a warm establishment y'all got here. So y'all jes' go on back to playin' n' dancin'. Go on.

No sooner has the Piano Player resumed playing . . .

JELLY: You call that playin'? That fool couldn't hit a piana wit' a brick.

45

The Piano Player slams down the piano lid and is about to go charging after Jelly when a large man—Sam— sitting at a table, signals him to stop.

SAM: Fo' a yella runt, you sho' be tawkin' a ton-ah-shit.

JELLY: Yeah well, I calls 'em as I see's 'em n' slays 'em as I go. Folks call me Sweet Papa Jelly Roll, finest piana man ever lived.

SAM *(Rising from table and crossing to Jelly)*: Folks call me Foot-in-yo'-Ass Sam. If you don't live up to yo' name title, I guess I'm gon' have to live up to mine.

Jelly crosses to the piano.

JACK: Ah, Jelly . . . you do know how to play?

SONG: *THAT'S HOW YOU JAZZ*

JELLY: *(Begins to play):*
I'LL SHOW YA HOW TO PLAY
LIKE FOLKS DOWN N'AWLINS WAY
SHOW YOU THE STYLISH FINGERS THEY HAS

Jelly plays a dazzling piano riff. The Crowd is instantly impressed.

OOOH WHAT A NOISE THEY MAKE
STOMP TILL THE WINDOWS SHAKE

START MIXIN'
C'MON N' GITCHA LICKS IN
OOH-OOH-OOH
THAT'S HOW YA JAZZ

In order to get goin', what I like to call "Sweet Papa Jelly's Jazz," ya got to start off with a lowdown foundation . . . *(He plays a phrase on the piano)*

MEN *(Imitating tubas)*:
BOM BOM
BOM BOM
BOM BOM
BOM BOM
BOM BOM
BOM BOM
BOM-BUH-DOM-DOM

JELLY: Then ya add some sweet-ass syncopation . . .

The Men, as tubas, continue their licks as the women add in . . .

WOMEN *(As banjos)*:
PLUNK-A-PLUNK
A-PLUNK-A-PLUNK-A-PLUNK
PLUNK-A-PLUNK
A-PLUNK-A-PLUNK-A-PLUNK
PLUNK-A-PLUNK
A-PLUNK-A-PLUNK-A-PLUNK
BIDDELEY-DIDDELEY-DUM
BIDDELEY-DIDDELEY-DUM

JELLY: Next, I need some bluesy "variations."

He plays a blues lick. Vocal tuba and banjo licks continue as the "horns" add in.

MEN/WOMEN *(As horns)*:
WAH-AAH
WAH-AAH
WAH-AAH
WAH-AAH

The three figures—tubas, banjos and horns—continue under Jelly's text.

JELLY: N' you can leave the melody to me.

Jelly begins to sing, with the Dance Hall Crowd as his vocal orchestra.

JELLY:

TAKE BUDDY BOLDEN'S BLUES
SOME CREOLE CURLICUES
ADD SOME STREET-RAG RAZZMATAZZ

CROWD *(Banjos only):*

BIDDELEY-DIDDELEY-DA
BIDDELEY-DIDDELEY-DA

JELLY;

THAT TUNE STRUT-STRUTS ALONG
JUST LIKE IT OWNS THE SONG
THEN YA HIT IT WITH A—

CROWD:

DO-WEE-DEE-LAH-DO
WHOOP-DE-DAH-DAH

JELLY:

THAT'S HOW YOU JAZZ
N' NOW THE TUNE IS GOIN'

WOMEN:

OOOH DADDY SING TO ME

JELLY:

GIMME SOME "UNNH"
OR IT—

CROWD:

DON'T MEAN A THING TO ME

JELLY:

WATER DON'T COME WETTA
PIANA MEN DON'T COME BETTA

CROWD:

UNH UNH UNH
C'MON LET'S JAZZ!

*The Crowd clears the floor and looks on in amazement
as Jelly uses tap or scat to illustrate jazz.*

CROWD:

THAT'S HOW YOU JAZZ!

Jelly tap/scat break.

CROWD:

THAT'S JAZZ!

Jelly tap/scat break.

CROWD:

THAT'S HOW YOU JAZZ!

Jelly tap break/scat.

CROWD:

THAT'S JAZZ!

*Jelly encourages the Dance Hall Crowd to join in. And they
do—cautiously at first, until the music and rhythms free them.
An exuberant dance of syncopation and scat ensues. Five
members of the Crowd form a vocal quintet at the piano.*

QUINTET/CROWD:

JAZZ!
JAZZ!
JAZZ!
OOOOH!
JAZZ!
JAZZ!
JAZZ!

QUINTET:
OOOOH!
JAZZ!
JAZZ!
JAZZ!

Tap/scat break—Jelly with the Crowd.

QUINTET:
OOOOH!

Tap/scat break—Jelly with the Crowd.

QUINTET:
OOOOOH!

WAH WAH-WAH
WAH-WAH
WAH-WAH

QUINTET/CROWD:
N' NOW THE TUNE IS GOIN'
THE WAH-WAH IS SHOWIN'
WATER DON'T COME WETTA
PIANA MEN DON'T COME BETTA
OOH OOH OOH
THAT'S HOW YA JAZZ

N' NOW THE TUNE IS GOIN'
THE WAH-WAH'S SHOWIN'

OOOOOH . . .
OOOOOH . . .
OOOOOH . . .
OOOOH-OOOOH

N' NOW THE TUNE IS GOIN'
OOH DADDY SING TO ME

GIMME SOME "UNNH"
OR IT DON'T MEAN A THING TO ME
WATER DON'T CCME WETTA
PIANA MEN DON'T COME BETTA
OOH OOH OOH
THAT'S HOW YOU JAZZ
OOH OOH OOH
THAT'S HOW YOU JAZZ
OOH OOH OOH
THAT'S HOW . . .
YOU . . .
JAZZ . . .
JAZZ . . .
JAZZ . . .
That's how you jazz!

Reprise.

CROWD:

OH-OH-OH
THAT'S HOW YOU JAZZ!
OH-OH-OH
THAT'S HOW YOU JAZZ!
OH-OH-OH
THAT'S HOW . . .
YOU . . .

The exuberant energy transforms into an invocatory jazz-prayer.

CROWD:

JAZZ
JAZZ

Lights out on Jelly and the Dance Hall. As Jack does the following scat/speech, the Crowd maintains the above invocation.

JACK: A brownskin gal in ah Sunday dress
WAS INSIDE OF JELLY'S SONG.
Sittin' down to a meal by yo' mama after bein' gone too long from home
WAS INSIDE OF JELLY'S SONG.
Standin' on some open road, not knowin' where you goin', but knowin' it's gotta be better than the pain you leavin' behind
WAS INSIDE OF JELLY'S SONG.
A "Feel good, head high, strut low" kinda song! A
"HIGH LIFE OR NO LIFE, YA STILL GOTTA LIVE
YO' LIFE" KINDA SONG.
N' everywhere we went, folks claimed us as their own.
N' Jelly's music was like Moses, partin' the water n' pavin' the way for . . .
Chi-ca-go!

SCENE 5

Chicago!

Drumroll.

VOICE-OVER: The Rooftop Garden, Chicago's sepia supper club, proudly presents Jelly Roll Morton n' his Red Hot Peppers!

SONG: THE CHICAGO STOMP (Instrumental)

Flashing lights. Blaring music. Jelly and the Red Hot Peppers, his orchestra, are revealed, jamming away. A Chicago Crowd dances exuberantly.
Lights out on Jelly and the Crowd, and up on the Chimney Man.

CHIMNEY MAN:

RECORD DEAL WITH RCA
TURN OUT SIX HIT TUNES A DAY
DON'T LET NOBODY GET IN YOUR WAY
DOIN' THE CHICAGO STOMP

Lights reveal Jelly, a Shoeshine Boy at his feet and the Chicago Crowd clamoring all around him. Off to one side, Jack.

JELLY: Them boys in the recordin' session didn't know what hit 'em when I let 'em know I was the instigator, the precreator n' the high-tone imaginator of J-A-Double-Z.
    Once I laid down how I'd come up with tonal variations, the shifts in syncopation, yet letting the melodic structure fly, they was too through. Know what I told 'em! "Play it the way I wrote it, or get out!"

As the Chicago Crowd laughs and applauds, lights out on Jelly and the Crowd and up on the Chimney Man.

CHIMNEY MAN:

PUT SOME NEW SUITS ON YOUR BACK
BUY A BIG NEW CADILLAC
TELL THE WORLD YOUR ASS AIN'T BLACK
DO THE CHICAGO STOMP

53

Lights reveal Jelly talking to a Reporter/Photographer and standing in front of his "Cadillac"—the Hunnies as the car's headlights and grille. Jack is in the background "buffing up the car."

JELLY: N'awlins born n' bred. But ya see what most folks don't understand is that my ancestors came directly from the shores of France. No coon stock in this Creole.

Jelly laughs and poses. As the camera goes "flash," lights out on Jelly, the Reporter, etc., and up on Chimney Man.

CHIMNEY MAN:

SLICK AS SOAP AND HARD AS STEEL
FIND NEW WAYS TO WHEEL AND DEAL
CAN'T GET HURT IF YOU DON'T FEEL
DO THE CHICAGO STOMP

Lights reveal Jelly sipping champagne as Jack, acting as Jelly's valet, cleans off his suit.

JELLY: Jack, I had to let them gangster boys know straight out that the way they nickel n' dime all the shine musicians in town was not gonna work with "The Roll." I told 'em fifteen hundred a night. N' guess what I got?

JELLY/JACK: Fifteen hundred a night!

The Chicago Crowd envelops Jelly. The dancing builds to a big finish. Jelly and his music have conquered Chicago.

CROWD *(Chanting):* Go Jelly go! Go Jelly go! *(Etc.)*

*On the Chimney Man's signal, lights out on the Chicago
Crowd as lights reveal Anita, young, beautiful, standing
by a piano. Jelly is irresistibly drawn to her.*

CHIMNEY MAN: Music flyin' n' money flowin'—life couldn't
be better for "The Roll." Ah, but a one-night gig in a
nearby town turns Jelly into jam. She's calling to you
Jelly—waiting to replay the day you two first met.

SCENE 6

Jelly n' Anita

*Lights up on Anita's Club—small and intimate, with a
piano, beaded curtains, etc. Anita abruptly turns to face
Jelly, who now has Jack at his side.*

ANITA: Piano man, you're late.
JELLY: Generally when folks first meet, they say "Hello."
ANITA: Greeting took place forty-five minutes ago. If you'd
wanted to partake, ya should have been here.
JELLY: Jack?
JACK: In Chicago, things don't start till we arrive.
ANITA: Word's come my way you're all the rage there. But
sugah, this ain't Chicago. It's Cal City, Illinois. N' here
we do things on time. If you think you can live with
that, we'll begin. Otherwise you can leave n' I'll look
elsewhere.
JELLY: You're openin' a new club?

She nods. He sits at the piano.

JELLY: Well, if you're lookin' for the best, there is no elsewhere.

ANITA: You know "Play the Music for Me?"

JELLY: I probably wrote it. *(Laughing and very pleased with himself)* Jack, did you hear what I say? "I probably wrote it." Jelly, Jelly, Jelly!

Jack indicates to Jelly that Anita is waiting for him to play. Jelly begins to play.

SONG: *PLAY THE MUSIC FOR ME*

ANITA:
> OOH SAY IT
> YEAH PLAY IT
> PLAY ME A MIDNIGHT KEY
> PLAY A SMOKY ROOM
> PLAY A HE AND A SHE
> OH—WOOWOOWEE
> OOH SUGAH
> PLAY THE MUSIC FOR ME
>
> OH SING IT
> YEAH SWING IT
> SWEET POSSIBILITY
> PLAY A SOFT CARESS
> PLAY A "MAYBE, LET'S SEE"
> NO GUARANTEE
> OOH SUGAH
> PLAY THE MUSIC FOR ME
>
> MUSIC IN THE STRUTTIN'
> OF A FINE LOOKIN' MAN
> MUSIC IN THE STROKIN'
> OF A SWEET-TALKIN' HAN'

MUSIC IN THE LYIN'
MUSIC IN THE LAUGHIN'
IN LOVIN' YOUR WOMAN LIKE NOBODY CAN
IT'S IN THE MUSIC
WHERE THE LOVIN' SHOULD BE
THE MUSIC'S IN THE LIVIN'
PLAY THE MUSIC FOR ME

*Jelly plays a piano solo playfully and seductively. Anita
starts to scat.*

ANITA:
SHA-BA-DE-BA-BE-BA . . .
JELLY: Not yet.

He plays a bit more. She starts to scat.

ANITA:
SHA-BA-DE-BA . . .
JELLY: Not yet! *(He plays some more)* Jump in there
anytime, Baby!
ANITA:
WHEN YOU'RE TALKIN'
YOU'RE TALKIN' THE MUSIC
WHEN YOU'RE WALKIN'
YOU'RE WALKIN' THE MUSIC
SUGAH, THAT'S THE WAY IT'S
GOTTA BE
THE MUSIC'S IN THE LIVIN'
PLAY ME THE MUSIC
THE MUSIC'S IN THE LIVIN'
PLAY THE MUSIC FOR ME

Jelly and Anita applaud one another, as does Jack.

ANITA: So piano man, you got a name?

JELLY *(Turning on the charm)*: You want to know my name? Jack, tell her who I am.

JACK: This is *the* Jelly Roll Morton. Lover of women, inventor of jazz and owner of twenty-seven suits.

JELLY: N' you are . . . ?

ANITA: Not interested. *(Anita turns to go)*

JELLY: Ha! As many looks as you been throwin'.

ANITA: Just 'cause I throw a look, n' you catch it, don't mean it had your name on it. *(To Jack)* But you, Sugah, you ain't tell Sweet Anita your name.

Anita pours it on thick, flirting with Jack, enjoying how much it's annoying Jelly.

JACK *(Rising to the occasion)*: Folks call me Jack the Bear.

ANITA: Is that B-E-A-R or B-A-R-E?

JACK: Both.

He and Anita laugh.

JELLY *(Pulling Anita aside)*: Wait—whoa. Anita come on now. Jack's like a brother to me, but . . . there's no comparison. *(Confidentially)* For one thing he's so . . .

ANITA: So what Jelly? So black? Sugah, if I'd wanted a white man, I'd get me the real thing, n' not some pale imitation thereof. 'Cause like the sayin' goes, "The blacker the berry, the sweeter the juice."

JELLY: You know Anita, when I first saw you, I said to myself, "Jelly, before you stands a real lady." I now see I was wrong. *(He turns to go)* Jack?

Jack reluctantly follows after him.

ANITA *(Calling after Jelly):* Oh is that what you lookin' for?
"A lady!" Someone who smiles n' pours tea n' agrees
with her man, no matter what. He says it's sunny, n'
even though it's pourin', she stands there smiling,
pretending to not be wet. If that's what you're lookin'
for, sugah I can tell you now, ain't nobody home.

JELLY: If you think "The Roll" is gonna stand here while
you—

ANITA *(Overlapping):* Now, if you lookin' for a woman . . .
(Seductively) Full-hipped n' sweet-lipped, who says what
she feels n' feels it to the bone, then maybe, just maybe
somebody might be home.

Provided the man inquiring loved the way he played
instead of the way he talked. If that's the case, I'd advise
you to knock soon, 'cause Sweet Anita has no intention
of waitin' around till you do.

*Just as Anita is about to exit through the beaded
curtain . . .*

JELLY: Knock, knock.

*Jelly and Anita embrace. Music underscore. As they kiss,
they strip down to their undergarments. Lights out on
Anita's club and up on the Hunnies pushing a large
curtained brass bed. Jelly and Anita fall into it.*

SONG: LOVIN' IS A LOWDOWN BLUES

HUNNIES:
THEY SAY THAT LOVIN' IS A LOWDOWN BLUES
YOU AIN'T GOT NUTHIN' BUT YOUR LIFE TO
    LOSE

WHEN YOU CAN'T STOP YOURSELF FROM
     LOVIN'
LOVIN' IS A LOWDOWN BLUES

*The Hunnies open the curtains to reveal Jelly and Anita
having a post-coital conversation.*

JELLY: Sweeeet-Anita. Sweet-Sweet-Anita. Never met a
woman quite like you. *(Beat)* Well . . . ain't you gonna
say you never met a man quite like me?

Anita says nothing.

JELLY: Anita, come on now, it's common knowledge, can't
nobody roll like "The Roll."

ANITA: Sugah, haven't you heard . . . men who talk about
how good they are, generally aren't.

Jelly starts to seduce her.

ANITA: Generally they aren't . . . but occasionally . . . they are.

The Hunnies close the curtains on Jelly and Anita.

HUNNIE TWO:
     SHE THINKS HE'S
     UNNH SO . . .
HUNNIE ONE:
     YEAH SO . . .
HUNNIE THREE:
     YOU KNOW . . .
HUNNIES:
     LIGHT MY FUSE
HUNNIE TWO:
     HE THINKS SHE'S
     YEAH SO . . .

HUNNIE ONE:
  UNNH SO . . .
HUNNIE THREE:
  JUST WHAT
HUNNIES:
  HE CAN USE
  UH-HUH
  LOVIN' IS A FUCK-YOU BLUES

The Hunnies open the curtains.

JELLY: Anita, I don't have time to be owning no club. "The Roll" has big plans. We talkin' European tours. Maybe even a pit stop in that hick burg New York. Everywhere I go, they gonna love themselves some "Roll."
ANITA: Talkin' big is one thing. Thinkin' big is what counts.
JELLY: Oh so now I don't know how to think.
ANITA: If you would just listen to what I'm—
JELLY *(Overlapping)*: No, you're the one who needs to listen, 'cause see "The Roll" has gotten quite far in this world. "The Roll" has been able to—
ANITA *(Cutting him off)*: Aww Jelly to hell with "The Roll." This bed ain't big enough for you n' all your titles. There's only room for Jelly n' Anita.
JELLY: You know woman you talk a whole lotta trash.
ANITA: Yeah well man, so do you.
JELLY *(Grabbing her)*: I ought to . . .
ANITA: You ought to what . . . ?

The Hunnies close the curtains.

HUNNIE THREE:
  THEY'RE SO EXCITABLE
HUNNIES:
  UH-HUH

HUNNIE THREE:
> THEY'RE SO DELIGHTABLE

HUNNIES:
> UH-HUH
> IT LOOKS LIKE NUTHIN' BUT GOOD TIMES
> NUTHIN' BUT GOOD NEWS
> LOVIN' IS A SWEET-ASS BLUES

The Hunnies open the curtains.

JELLY: *"Va! Va!"* She told me to go, Anita. Said I was dirt. "You are not Creole." I sat on those steps, waiting for her to forgive me, let me in. She never did. *"Va. Va."*

Anita kisses him long and hard.

ANITA: Don't none of that matter now, 'cause I'm your home.

After a beat . . .

JELLY: Anita?
ANITA: Hmm?
JELLY: What you think of the name, "Jelly N' Anita's Midnight Inn?"

HUNNIE ONE:
> OOOOH
> WOH-WOH-WOH-WOH
> OOOOH
> WOH-WOH-WOH-WOH

ANITA *(During the above)*: Oooh Jelly, the place I've found, you are going to love.
JELLY: Wait a minute. You've already picked out the club.
ANITA: I see a baby grand piano, crystal chandeliers. My man deserves nuthin' but the best.

As the Hunnies sing, Jelly and Anita "make love."

HUNNIE TWO:
> BUT WHEN IT DIES . . .
> THE WAY IT DOES . . .
> AIN'T NO SURPRISE . . .

HUNNIES:
> LOVIN' IS A SLY-DOG BLUES

Jelly and Anita's lovemaking transforms into a fight.

ANITA *(Swinging at Jelly)*: You no-count-two-bit-two-timin'-son-of-a-bitch!

JELLY *(Overlapping)*: Anita . . . Anita, wait—whoa . . . Anita calm down n' listen. 'Cause see I've written hundreds of songs, each special in their own way.

ANITA: What's that got to do with us?

JELLY: Every once in a while, a song comes along n' it's from this whole other place way deep down inside. That's the kinda song you are.

ANITA: Oh I see. N' so regardless of how many other songs or bitches pass through "The Roll's" hands, that's alright. 'Cause I'm still your "one special song."

JELLY: Exactly. *(He moves in to kiss her)*

ANITA: Jelly you're good. You're real good. But like my mama used to say, "Jes' 'cause a man smiles while servin' shit don't mean it don't smell."

JELLY: You and yo' mama missed the point. *(Begins to get dressed)*

ANITA: Oh no sugah, your point was real clear. Just so long as you understand that that door swings both ways.

JELLY: What's that supposed to mean?

ANITA: You've been expanding your musical repertoire, well so have I.

JELLY: Shame on you, Anita. Sayin' you was with some man, just to get back at me.

ANITA: What makes you think it was a lie?

JELLY: Anita, a man knows things 'bout his woman that she don't know about herself. Like it or not woman, I got your game.

ANITA: Like it or not man, I got yours.

JELLY: Nobody's got "The Roll's" game. No sir, not "The Roll." But as far as bitches go, you come pretty close. Gotta go.

He stands to go, oblivious to the impact his last statement has had on her.

HUNNIES:

    THEY SAY THAT LOVIN' IS A LOWDOWN BLUES
    YOU AIN'T GOT NUTHIN' BUT YOUR LIFE TO
        LOSE
    WHEN YOU CAN'T STOP YOURSELF FROM
        LOVIN'

ANITA: Jelly?

JELLY: Hmm?

ANITA: You gonna be seein' Jack?

JELLY: Yeah, we hangin' . . .

ANITA: Well, will you give him my best.

Anita kisses Jelly long and hard. On the last line of the song, Anita and Jelly stare at each.

HUNNIES:

    LOVIN' IS A SLY-DOG
    SWEET-ASS,
    FUCK-YOU
    LOWDOWN DIRTY BLUES

*Lights isolate Jelly, clearly affected by the scene.
Chimney Man enters holding a large gift box and
crosses to Jelly.*

CHIMNEY MAN: Remember how you felt Jelly? I mean the
very idea that Anita would choose someone like Jack
over someone like you. The very idea!
  Remember how you waited till the opening of your
club? *(He presents Jelly with the box)* Remember?

Jelly takes box and exits.

SCENE 7

Jelly and Anita's Midnight Inn

*Jelly and Anita's Midnight Inn, a stylish nightclub. Jack,
in dapper attire, is surveying the place when Anita
enters, also in elegant attire.*

JACK: *(Ad lib singing from "Somethin' More")*
ANITA *(Upon seeing Jack):* Well I do declare, let me take a
gander at Mr. Jack the Bear.
JACK: Pretty, huh? Oh n' check out the shoes . . .
  (Confidentially) Straight from the bovine's butt to my
feet, with no hand-me-down stops along the way.

*Jelly appears at entrance of the club holding the box
given to him by the Chimney Man. He silently watches
the following exchange.*

JACK: Aww but now, ain't you one to put the peacock to
shame.

ANITA: Lookin' so good, I gots to be illegal. One touch a get ya five to ten.

JACK: Then I guess I'm gonna be servin' life.

Jack and Anita laugh and hug. Jelly enters the club.

JACK *(Seeing Jelly):* Jelly my man, you git a load of that crowd? *(He laughs)*

ANITA: You're late. *(She starts to leave)*

JACK *(Catching her and bringing them all together):* Come on, Sweet Anita, lay off. Jes' for tonight, everybody loves everybody.

JELLY: I couldn't agree more.

He presents Jack with the box.

JACK: Awww Jelly man, no!

JELLY: Go on, open it!

Jack takes from the box a bright red doorman's coat.

JACK: I don't understand . . .

JELLY: Well ya see back in N'awlins, Countess Willie Piazza used to have this colored midget that worked as her doorman. N' this white fella one time told me, he said "Jelly, I can't explain it, but havin' a li'l nigga in a red coat opening that door, makes me feel like I belong."

Jack starts a slow laugh which grows. Jelly returns the laughter.

JACK: Jelly, man you crazy man.

ANITA: Jelly, please.

JACK: She thinks you're serious. Jelly n' me always pullin' shit like this on each other. My ace-boon-coon.

JELLY: I'll be the ace n' you be the coon.

GEORGE C. WOLFE AND SUSAN BIRKENHEAD

Jelly and Jack laugh.

ANITA: Jelly just stop it!

JELLY *(Overlapping; ignoring Anita):* After all, we want folks to feel like they belong? Well we got the li'l nigga—n' a sweet one to boot. "Blacker the berry . . .", so forth n' so on. N' we got the red coat. So what seems to be the problem?

JACK: Jelly man, why you doin' this?

JELLY: We share everything. What's yours is mine n' mine, yours. N' seein' as I'm the one who's got everything— the name, the money, the talent, the women . . . or should I say woman—you ain't got shit! So be a good nigga n' put on the coat.

The tension is broken as Jack throws the coat on the ground and then exits. Jelly crosses to the piano and begins to pick out a tune.

ANITA: Well now, I bet "The Roll" is feelin' real good. I bet he's flyin' high. Who was it Jelly? Was it some ho'? Or maybe it was yo' Grandma kickin' your ass out.

JELLY: You watch your mouth!

ANITA: Who hurt you so hard n' cut you so deep that the second you feel any kinda pain, you don't think, you don't feel, you just lash out.

Makin' you think there was somethin' goin' on between Jack n' me was wrong. But it was nuthin' compared to what you just did, to Jack, to me, to us. *(Pulling Jelly away from the piano)* Are you listening to me?

JELLY: You better go see 'bout your boy. He looked kinda upset.

ANITA: Don't do this. Don't treat me like I don't matter.

67

She stops, waits for Jelly to say something. He doesn't.
She then turns to go.

JELLY: Anita wait . . .

Anita stops. He picks up the red coat.

JELLY: Jack forgot his coat.

Music cue. She exits. Lights isolate Jelly.

SONG: DR. JAZZ

JELLY *(With an edge):*
    LISTEN PEOPLE HERE COMES DOCTOR JAZZ
    HE'S GOT GLORY ALL AROUND HIM, YES HE
        HAS
    WHEN THE WORLD GOES WRONG
    N' YOU GOT THE BLUES
    HE'S THE MAN WHAT MAKES YOU GET OUT
    BOTH YOUR DANCIN' SHOES

On Jelly's signal, lights reveal the Crowd as a Chorus of
Coons, in white lips and red doormen's jackets and caps.

CHORUS OF COONS *(Spoken):*
    Front n' center the inventor of jazz!
    Got the magic—
JELLY: Yes he has!
CHORUS OF COONS *(Sung):*
    AIN'T NO MEDICINE KNOWN TO MAN
JELLY/CHORUS OF COONS:
    CAN MAKE YOU FEEL GOOD LIKE THE DOCTOR
        CAN
CHORUS OF COONS: Only name that you need to know—

JELLY:

WORLD'S GREATEST ONE-MAN SHOW

CHORUS OF COONS:

EVEN THE DEVIL, WHOEVER HE WAS
COULDN'T PLAY JAZZ THE WAY JELLY DOES
HELLO CENTRAL, GIVE ME GIVE ME DOCTOR
JAZZ

JELLY:

HELLO CENTRAL, GIVE ME DOCTOR JAZZ
GOT GLORY ALL AROUND HIM, YES HE HAS
C'MON ON YOUR FEET N' SWING WITH THE
ROLL
FEEL HIS RHYTHM RIPPIN' THROUGH YA
RIGHT DOWN TO YOUR SOUL

SO SPREAD THE WORD WHEREVER YOU MAY
GO
YOU'VE SEEN THE LIGHT TONIGHT N' NOW
YOU KNOW
BLAZE HIS NAME ACROSS THE SKY
FLAMING LETTERS TEN FEET HIGH
"J.R. MORTON, MISTER DOCTOR JAZZ"

*As Jelly dances, his rage releases itself as a manic
"showstopper"—driving himself and the Chorus of
Coons in a dance break that is as exuberant as it is
emotionally raw.*

JELLY:

HELLO WORLD
You can call me Jelly
WHO DO YOU LOVE?

CHORUS OF COONS: Jelly!

JELLY: Louder!

CHORUS OF COONS:
> EVERYBODY LOVES THEIR DOCTOR JAZZ!

Lights reveal Chimney Man.

CHORUS OF COONS:
> DOCTOR JAZZ

On Chimney Man's signal, Jelly sees a face in the void—Anita.

CHORUS OF COONS:
> DOCTOR JAZZ

On Chimney Man's signal, Jelly sees a second face in the void—Jack.

CHORUS OF COONS:
> DOCTOR—

On Chimney Man's signal, Jelly sees—Gran Mimi, ordering him to go.

CHORUS OF COONS:
> IT'S DOCTOR JAZZ!

Blackout.

Chimney Man (Keith David) and Jelly Roll Morton (Gregory Hines).

"Michigan Water."

"The Creole Way"

Gregory Hines (center), "That's How You Jazz."

Young Jelly (Savion Glover) and Jelly Roll Morton (Gregory Hines),
"The Whole World's Waitin' to Sing Your Song."

"Lovin' is a Lowdown Blues."

"Shootin' the Agaite."

*Anita (Tonya Pickins), Jack the Bear (Stanley Wayne Mathis) and
Jelly Roll Morton (Gregory Hines).*

*The Melrose Brothers (Don Johanson, Gordon Joseph Weiss) flank
Jelly Roll Morton (Gregory Hines).*

*Jelly Roll Morton (Gregory Hines) and Jack the Bear
(Stanley Wayne Mathis).*

ACT TWO

SCENE I

The Chimney Man Takes Charge

Lights reveal Jelly and the Chimney Man posed as they were at the end of Act One.

CHIMNEY MAN *(Laughs):* You know Jelly, you're having quite the night. "No coon stock in this Creole." "Be a good nigga n' put on the coat." N' my all-time favorite: "I invented jazz."

JELLY: Before there was Jelly, there was a bunch of shines moanin' the blues n' a ton of hacks bangin' on keys.
(Mimes piano playing)
Tonka-tonka-tonka-tonka-tonk!
Ooooh baby-baby—I's got the blues.
I'm the one who took the shit n' made it soar—maintain the melody, throw in a break, add a riff, shift the syncopation, shift the syncopation. Jelly's jazz, Jelly's jazz.
Ask any of them fools who came before me n' they

71

haven't got a clue. Ask any of the ones who came after n' they'll tell you it all started with me.

CHIMNEY MAN: It all started with you, huh? Nothing but savages beatin' with sticks. N' then lo n' behold, there came forth "The Roll."

JELLY: Listen Shine, let me tell you one damn thing—

CHIMNEY MAN *(Overlapping)*: No let me tell you!

On Chimney's signal, Jelly freezes.

CHIMNEY MAN: We're goin' on a journey Jelly, you n' me. To the deepest, darkest part of the night. It's a sweet little song we're gonna sing. N' once the music starts there's no turning back. First stop, New York City!
  Spotlight!

On Chimney Man's signal, lights out on Jelly. Music underscore.

CHIMNEY MAN: Now it's true that in Chicago they loved themselves some Roll. But when he left there and went to New York, it was Filet of Soul, a la "The Roll."

SCENE 2

The New York Suite

A glorious fanfare. Blazing lights. New York City. Lights reveal the Hunnies and Chimney Man done over stylish and slickin'.

SONG: GOOD OLE NEW YORK

HUNNIES:
GOOD OLE NEW YORK
OUR KIND OF TOWN
CHIMNEY MAN:
BIG TIME BUCKS AND BROADWAY PALACES
HUNNIES:
HOCK YOUR SOUL AND HIT THE HEIGHTS
CHIMNEY MAN:
FRONT PAGE PICTURES IN THE PAPERS AND—
HUNNIES:
PRESTO! THERE'S YOUR NAME IN LIGHTS

An overly zealous Jelly appears with Variety *newspaper in hand.*

JELLY:
NEW YORK LOOK OUT!
I own you starting now
I'LL MAKE YOU SHOUT
Stand back 'cause I know how!
CHIMNEY MAN/HUNNIES:
STEP RIGHT UP YOUR DREAM IS WAITING
IT'S TIME TO POP THE CORK
WELCOME TO GOOD OLE NEW YORK

As Jelly "rides" the A train.

CHIMNEY MAN/HUNNIES:
UPTOWN
HUNNIE ONE:
YOU WANNA GO WHERE
THEY KNOW HOW TO SYNCOPATE
CHIMNEY MAN/HUNNIES:
UPTOWN

HUNNIE TWO:
> HOME OF THE "YEAH"
> DO WE HAVE TO ELUCIDATE?

HUNNIE THREE:
> THE PLACE WHERE THE PACE
> IS STRICTLY JAZZ

Lights reveal the interior of a Harlem Club and the Harlem Folk, elegantly attired.

CHIMNEY MAN/HUNNIES/HARLEM FOLK:
> HARLEM!

The Harlem Folk break into exuberant dancing.

CHIMNEY MAN/HUNNIES/HARLEM FOLK:
> DO-WAH DO-WAH DO-WAH DO-WAY
> WAH WAH-WAH WAH-WAY

SONG: TOO LATE, DADDY

JELLY:
> I'LL SHOW YOU HOW TO PLAY
> LIKE FOLKS DOWN N'AWLINS WAY
> SHOW YOU THE STYLISH MUSIC THEY HAS
> OOH WHAT A NOISE THEY MAKE
> STOMP TILL THE WINDOWS SHAKE
> FOLKS MIXIN'
> C'MON N' GIT YOUR LICKS IN
> OOH-OOH

Tap/scat break.

JELLY:
> OOH-OOH

Tap/scat break.

JELLY:

THAT'S HOW . . .

YOU . . .

Jelly's rhythm is replaced by a swinging rhythm which all the Harlem Folk begin to dance to.

HARLEM FOLK:

. . . JAZZ!

YOU'RE TOO LATE DADDY
WE'RE SWINGIN' A WHOLE NEW SONG
IT'S GOT US JUMPIN'
N' SWINGIN' THE WHOLE NIGHT LONG

WOMEN:

IT'S A REET SWEET BEAT
THAT'S GOIN' 'ROUND

MEN:

THE JIM-JAM JIVE
THE SLAM-JAM SOUND

HARLEM FOLK:

YOU'RE TOO LATE DADDY
WE'RE SWINGIN' TO A WHOLE NEW SOUND

JELLY: Maybe you didn't hear me. The name is Jelly Roll Morton . . . the inventor of jazz.

HARLEM FOLK:

WHO NEEDS JELLY WHEN WE GOT LOUIS?

CROWD MEMBER TWO: *(Solo scat a la Louis Armstrong)*

JELLY: Louis Armstrong! That coon. That baboon.

HARLEM FOLK:

WHO NEEDS JELLY WHEN WE GOT THE DUKE?

CROWD MEMBER SIX: *(Solo scat a la Duke Ellington)*

JELLY: Duke Ellington ain't good enough to—

HARLEM FOLK:
   BUT WE GOT BASIE!
CROWD MEMBER NINE: *(Solo scat a la Count Basie)*
HARLEM FOLK:
   WE'RE SWINGIN' . . . TO A WHOLE NEW SOUND!

The Harlem Folk break into a raucous dance, driving Jelly off to the side.

HARLEM FOLK:
   IT'S TOO LATE DADDY
   WE'RE SWINGIN' SWINGIN' SWINGIN'
   TO A WHOLE NEW SONG
JELLY: I'll be back, n' when I do you'll be throwin' me a parade!
CROWD MEMBER THREE: Honey, you better go downtown where they don't know what real music is!

The Hunnies and Chimney Man reappear. They sing as Jelly struts "Downtown."

CHIMNEY MAN/HUNNIES:
   DOWNTOWN
HUNNIE ONE:
   YOU BETTER GO WHERE THE
   DEALS AND THE DOLLARS ARE
CHIMNEY MAN/HUNNIES:
   DOWNTOWN
HUNNIE TWO:
   MEET WITH THE CATS WITH THE
   HATS AND THE FAT CIGARS
HUNNIE THREE:
   WHERE THE NAME OF THE GAME
   IS "WHO'S ON TOP"

Lights reveal four Tin Pan Alley office doors.

HUNNIES:

TIN PAN ALLEY!

Jelly sings and plays the piano as if auditioning.

JELLY:

I'M THE MAN YOU ALL BEEN WAITIN' FOR
I'M THE BEST THERE IS, THERE AIN'T NO MORE
WHEN IT COMES TO JAZZ, "THE ROLL" IS IT
WAIT . . . LOOK! THIS TUNE S A HIT!

(Demonstrating piano licks)

COUPLE OF FRILLS
COUPLE OF FILLS
GIVE 'EM A GLISS
NOW LISTEN TO THIS
WOW!
POW!

From behind one of the doors pop the Melrose Brothers—Frank and Al—fast-talking, fast-dancing, ex-vaudevillians turned music publishers, holding a contract and pen.

MELROSE BROTHERS: Yeah-yeah-yeah-yeah-yeah-yeah-yeah-yeah . . .

SONG: *THAT'S THE WAY WE DO THINGS
IN NEW YAWK*

FRANK:

JELLY BABY
SO YOU'RE SAYIN' YOU WANNA GO FAR?

AL: Then sign on the dotted line . . .

FRANK:

>   AIN'T NO MAYBE, BABY
>   WE'RE GONNA MAKE YOU A STAR!

AL: So sign on the dotted line . . .

FRANK:

>   DEPEND ON FRANK N' AL . . .

AL: The leading publishers . . .

FRANK:

>   THE MELROSE BROTHERS, PAL

AL: Of colored music.

JELLY:

>   ALRIGHT FELLAS
>   WHAT MONEY WE TALKIN'?

FRANK:

>   THE MINOR POINTS WE WON'T DISCUSS

AL:

>   WE DO FOR YOU, YOU DO FOR US

JELLY:

>   WON'T TALK MONEY? C'MON DO I
>   LOOK LIKE A FOOL?

MELROSE BROTHERS:

>   YA KNOW WE'RE GONNA DO RIGHT BY
>   YOU!

JELLY:

>   I DONE BETTER
>   PITCHIN' PENNIES AND HUSTLIN' POOL!

MELROSE BROTHERS:

>   C'MON, WE'RE GONNA DO RIGHT BY YOU!
>   THEY'RE BOUND TO SCREW YOU DOWN THE
>   PIKE
>   WHY NOT BE SCREWED BY FOLKS YOU LIKE?

AL:

YOU JUST GIVE US A TUNE WE CAN DANCE TO

FRANK:

YOU GET TO SEE YOUR NAME IN LIGHTS

AL:

WE GET TO KEEP THE COPYRIGHTS

MELROSE BROTHERS:

SIGN!

JELLY:

NO!

MELROSE BROTHERS:

SIGN!

JELLY:

NO!

MELROSE BROTHERS:

OR TAKE A WALK
'CAUSE THAT'S THE WAY WE DO THINGS

JELLY:

WELL THAT'S NOT THE WAY THAT "THE ROLL"
DOES THINGS

MELROSE BROTHERS:

THAT'S THE WAY WE DO THINGS IN NEW YORK

The Melrose Brothers exit through two separate doors.

HUNNIES: You think they're bad, Jelly, you ain't seen nuthin'
yet.

*Two Gangsters enter, Nick and Gus. Lights out on the
Chimney Man and the Hunnies.*

NICK:

GO ON PLAY
PLAY A TUNE, MR. PIANO MAN
THE NAME'S NICK

GUS:

    N' GUS

NICK:

    YOU PLAY, YOU PLAY FOR US

GUS:

    WE TELL YOU

    WHAT N' WHO

    YOU'LL BE PLAYING FOR

    WE'RE SO TO SPEAK YOUR "PATRONS OF DE

        ARTS"

NICK:

    LIKE WE SAID

    PLAY A TUNE, MR. PIANO MAN

GUS:

    PLAY ANY CLUB OR HALL

NICK:

    GUESS WHAT, WE OWN 'EM ALL

GANGSTERS:

    YOU WANNA MAKE IT BIG HERE

    SIDDOWN, WE'LL TALK

They offer Jelly a chair. He doesn't move.

GANGSTERS:

    SIDDOWN, WE'LL TALK

Jelly doesn't move.

GUS: Jelly, listen, let us give you a piece of advice or you'll be
outta here yesterday. You step on someone's feet, n'
nigga you don't eat.

JELLY *(Exploding):* Now you listen n' listen good! I'm not
some wooly-headed coon dancin' n' catchin' coins on a
corner. When you're prepared to deal with me as a
Creole, we'll talk.

NICK: What's he tawkin' 'bout?

GUS: Creole, shmeole! There's kikes, niggers n' wops. I leave anybody out?

NICK: Nope.

GANGSTERS: That's the way we do things in New York.

JELLY: I don't need any of them. After all . . .

I'M THE ONE YOU SPORTS CAN'T WAIT TO SEE

Lights reveal the Gangsters, the Harlem Folk and the Hunnies, who become the doors of the city.

PEOPLE OF NEW YORK:

DOOR SLAM! DOOR SLAM!

JELLY:

IF YOU TALKIN' JAZZ YOU TALKIN' ME

PEOPLE OF NEW YORK:

DOOR SLAM! DOOR SLAM!

JELLY:

GONNA TURN THIS CITY—

PEOPLE OF NEW YORK:

SLAM! SLAM! SLAM!

The Chimney Man struts on a la Cab Calloway.

CHIMNEY MAN:

EVERYWHERE HE TURNS

HUNNIES:

EVERYWHERE HE TURNS

CHIMNEY MAN:

EVERYTHING HE TRIES

HUNNIES:

EVERYTHING HE TRIES

HUNNIES/PEOPLE OF NEW YORK:
DOOR SLAM! DOOR SLAM!
DOOR SLAM! DOOR SLAM!
CHIMNEY MAN:
FROM THE RITZIEST CLUBS
TO THE RAUNCHIEST DIVES
HUNNIES/PEOPLE OF NEW YORK:
DOOR SLAM! DOOR SLAM!
DOOR SLAM! DOOR SLAM!
DOOR SLAM!
ALONE . . . ALONE . . .
CHIMNEY MAN:
ALONE

*The People of New York fade away. In isolated
light, Jelly. As the Chimney Man talks, Jelly dances/scats
his mounting frustration. The Hunnies maintain
a chant.*

HUNNIES:
HOW YA DOIN' MR. PIANO MAN . . .
HOW YA DOIN' MR. PIANO MAN . . .
CHIMNEY MAN: "Who needs Jelly when we got Louis?"
"Come on, we're gonna do right by you." "Too late
Daddy, we're swingin' to a whole new sound." "Door
slam! Door slam!" "You step on someone's feet, n' nigga
you don't eat." "Siddown, we'll talk." "Siddown, we'll
talk." "Siddown, we'll talk."

*Music out. Lights reveal a New York Railroad Flat—
a piano covered with crumpled sheet music; a radio on
top of the piano; etc.*

DANCE: JELLY IN ISOLATION

Jelly, alone, overwhelmed by the silence, begins to dance, trying to find his rhythm. Anxiety builds until he explodes and is left standing powerless. All of a sudden, he hears a rhythm. It's Young Jelly. The two engage in a dance of innocence, celebration and triumph. Jelly has regained his confidence. He crosses to his piano and is about to begin writing when the Chimney Man appears and clicks on the radio.

ANNOUNCER *(Voice-over of Chimney Man):* Alright Mrs. Mary Joe Jones of Jones, Indiana, for the all-important bonus round, who invented jazz?

Jelly sits up and begins to listen intently.

ANNOUNCER *(Voice-over):* Was it "A," Paul Whiteman, "B," W. C. Handy or "C," Jelly Roll Morton? You now have five seconds.

JELLY: You got that right! Jelly Roll Morton!

CONTESTANT *(Voice-over):* Oh—ah—ooo—let me see, now. "A," Paul Whiteman.

Buzzer sound.

ANNOUNCER *(Voice-over):* Aw, sorry Mary Joe . . .

JELLY *(Overlapping):* Sorry, Mary Joe!

ANNOUNCER *(Voice-over):* . . . it's "B," W. C. Handy. Next week on *Ripley's Believe It or Not,* the bonus jackpot will be worth . . .

JELLY: No! No!

Jelly switches off the radio and sits at the piano, totally defeated.

CHIMNEY MAN:
>THE PAIN IS REAL
>RELAX N' DON'T FIGHT IT
>TAKE WHAT YOU FEEL
>Now go ahead, write it.

Jelly begins to play as if writing a song. Isolated light reveals Anita, now many years older than when last seen.

SONG: THE LAST CHANCE BLUES

ANITA:
>ONE DAY THE WORLD IS SITTIN'
>IN YOUR SWEET YOUNG HAND
>THEN ALL AT ONCE YOU TURN AROUND
>N' THERE YOU STAND
>A FACE YOU BARELY RECOGNIZE
>THE LITTLE LINES AROUND THE EYES
>TALKIN' 'BOUT THE LAST CHANCE BLUES

JELLY:
>LEGS ARE GETTIN' SLOWER
>N' I GOT NOWHERE TO GO
>MONEY GETTIN' LOWER
>N' PEOPLE SAYIN' NO
>BROKEN DREAMS N' WASTED BETS
>NOW AND THEN A FEW REGRETS
>TALK ABOUT YOUR LAST CHANCE BLUES

ANITA:
>AIN'T IT FUN . . .

JELLY:
>AIN'T IT GREAT . . .
>DRESSED TO THE NINES

ANITA:

N' TEN YEARS OUT OF DATE

JELLY:

NEW YORK TIMES SAYS
I'M YESTERDAY'S NEWS
I GOT THE LAST CHANCE BLUES

ANITA:

WHAT IF I WHISPERED LOW
"SWEET MAN, I NEED YOU SO"
JUST ONCE KEPT MY FINGER OFF THE FUSE?
BUT NO, I HAD TO FIGHT
PROVE I WAS RIGHT
WELL THAT'S THE THING ABOUT
THE LAST CHANCE BLUES

JELLY:

WHAT IF
I NEVER LIED
WHAT IF JUST ONCE I TRIED TO SAY
HOW I REALLY FEEL
'STEAD OF PUSHIN' HER AWAY
IF I'D KNOWN
HOW MUCH I HAD TO LOSE
I WOULDN'T BE SINGIN'
THE LAST CHANCE BLUES

JELLY/ANITA: *(Scat verse)*

JELLY:

IF I

ANITA:

IF I SAW HIM

JELLY:	ANITA:
SAW HER THERE	STANDING THERE

JELLY:

LOOKIN' HARDER THAN

JELLY:	ANITA:
HELL	MEAN AS HELL
I DON'T CARE	I WOULDN'T CARE
I'D	I WOULD TELL HIM, "HEY
MAKE HER LISTEN	YOU GOTTA LISTEN TO ME"
HEY BABY	SHOUT SO HE COULD HEAR
I LOVE YOU	SWEET MAN I LOVE YOU

JELLY/ANITA:

DON'T MAKE ME SING THE
LAST CHANCE BLUES
NOW THAT I KNOW WHAT I COULD LOSE . . .

JELLY:

I DON'T WANNA SING THE . . .

JELLY/ANITA:

LAST CHANCE BLUES

The lights crossfade to reveal . . .

SCENE 3

The Last Chance

A small-time restaurant—a few tables; a piano. Anita sits, reflective, as Jelly slowly enters the place. Music underscore.

JELLY: Anita?

ANITA *(Incredulous)*: Jelly?

She laughs, rushes to him. They embrace one another, like old friends.

ANITA: Just look at you.
JELLY: No, look at you!

They both feel themselves going to "that place" and decide to pull back.

JELLY/ANITA: So . . .
ANITA: . . . been a long time.
JELLY: Yep. See ya got yo'self a new place.
ANITA: Nuthin' like "Jelly N' Anita's Midnight Inn," but it feeds me n' a few other folks.
JELLY: Nice piano.
ANITA: N' from time to time I sing me a tune.

Jelly applauds.

ANITA: I don't know why you're applauding. You never encouraged me before.
JELLY: I said a lot of things back then. But so did you. Lord knows I tried to git along with you.
ANITA: You! Sugah, I know I'm goin' to heaven after all the hell you put me through.

They laugh.

JELLY: I always loved the way you said "Sugah." Even when you was evil, it still sounded sweet.

They smile at one another. Chimney Man enters to observe the scene. After a beat . . .

JELLY: Anita?
ANITA: Hmm?

JELLY: Is that red beans n' rice I smell?

ANITA *(Laughs):* Umhm. N' on Fridays, it's Gumbo a la Anita.

JELLY: Enough to make a person wanna hang his hat n' stick around for a few.

ANITA: Not to mention a sign out front sayin' "Mr. Jelly Roll Morton Appearin' Here Tonight!"

JELLY *(Playful):* Seein' as I am the inventor of jazz . . . so forth n' so on, what kinda pay we tawkin'?

ANITA: All the Gumbo a la Anita you can take.

JELLY: Well now, good gumbo outside of N'awlins is mighty hard to find. But it can be done. N' in my life I've seen a whole lotta signs sayin' "Jelly Roll Morton Appearing Tonight."

But the thing that could make a person really consider hangin' for a few, is the "a la Anita." Ah, could you tell me how's that served?

ANITA: Hot. N' over a bed of rice.

JELLY: He'p me Jesus! Already dreamin' 'bout seconds n' I ain't finished firsts.

ANITA: As "The Roll" used to say, "Nuthin' to it, but to do it."

Music fades out.

JELLY: Ya know, Anita—you're the closest I've ever come to feelin' like I belong.

Just as they are about to hug, Jack enters.

JACK: Look out! I done died n' gone to hell!

Anita and Jelly turn to find Jack standing before them.

JACK: Got's to be hell, 'cause where else but would I run into "The Roll!"

Jack rushes and hugs Jelly, who is instantly on edge.

JACK: Jelly! My man! I don't believe it! Anita did you know 'bout this?

ANITA: I'm as surprised as you.

JACK: Damn it's good to see you. Why jes' the other night me n' Sweet Anita was tawkin' 'bout all the "way backs" that are long gone. I remember thinkin', "Damn what mess Jelly's gone n' got us into now. Things can't git no worse!" I now realize, things was never better. Wish I'd known it at the time. Woulda enjoyed 'em even more!

He looks to Anita who motions him to "get lost."

JACK: Well . . . let me let you two talk, while I take care of a few things. You are stickin' around? Anita?

ANITA: We're workin' on it.

JACK: Well work away. *(As he exits, sings)*
Ha-ha!
GOT NO LUNCH
AIN'T GOT NO DINNER
POCKETS THIN

ANITA *(Laughing):* Some things never change.

JELLY *(With an edge):* N' they never will.

ANITA: Now about you performing, I can't afford neon. But I figure we rig up a few lights, make a big sign n'—

JELLY *(Exploding):* Goddamnit Anita, shut up!

ANITA: Did I miss something?

JELLY: N' don't try n' act like you don't know what's goin' on. What the hell is he doing here?

ANITA: Don't do this Jelly. Don't come back talking the same kinda trash that killed what we had.

89

JELLY *(Overlapping):* Things happen. From the past. Things you've said n' done that over time, you regret. N' then "Bam," some shit goes n' hits you in the face n' you realize, Jelly, Jelly, Jelly, you were right all along.

ANITA: Oh, so, let me get this right? I've lived my entire life, probably even arranged the Depression, so that after we broke up, I moved to California, bumped into Jack, he needed work. N' for years we've been plugging away, barely gettin' by, just in case someday you might happen to walk through that door n' I could say, "Ooh Jelly, I don't love you. I never did. I love Jack. Sweet Jack! Hot Jack! Black Jack!"

JELLY: Once a ho', always a ho'.

Anita slaps Jelly.

ANITA: After all this time, is that all I am to you?

Jelly is silent.

ANITA: For once in your life Jelly, admit your pain n' quit treatin' people like they was dirt. Especially the ones you love n' the ones who love you. *(After a beat)* Dear God, you don't know how.

Jelly turns away, helpless.

ANITA: Listen Jelly, times are hard n' in honor of what once was, the offer still stands about you working here. It's decent pay, meals included.

JELLY *(Deeply wounded but determined to not show it):* Thank you very kindly Anita, but that won't be necessary. I'm out here on big business. A new club in Los Angeles, on Central Avenue, wants me to headline. Details of the deal are still being worked out. N' the motion picture people have expressed interest in my life story.

ANITA: I'm glad to hear it.

JELLY: So you see "Sweet Anita," I don't need your charity . . . n' I don't need you.

ANITA: Oh, Sugah . . .

Anita crosses to him and attempts to embrace him; he freezes up.

ANITA *(Sensing his resistance):* All my best. *(She exits)*

CHIMNEY MAN: Very good, Jelly. Brilliant. Just when you're about to get things right, you go n' say some stupid shit like you just did. Why, Jelly?

JELLY: I don't know.

CHIMNEY MAN: Why, Jelly?

JELLY: I don't know why. You tell me. Tell me goddamnit!

Jelly breaks down. Jack quickly appears.

JACK: Where's Anita?

JELLY *(Pulling himself together):* She's ah . . . off doin' . . .

JACK: Jelly, man what's wrong?

JELLY: Nuthin'.

JACK: Funny huh, us back together after all these years. You n' me n' Sweet Anita. So what can I get you? Me n' Sweet Anita got ourselves a cook, n' Jel-leee, the man can throw down a mean batch of red beans!

Jelly takes a beat and then looks Jack dead in the eye.

JELLY: Jack, when are you gonna learn the only thing a nigga can do for me is scrub my steps n' shine my shoes.

CHIMNEY MAN: Why, Jelly?

The club fades away.

JACK: Was I a nigga when we was on the road together?

CHIMNEY MAN: Why?

JACK: Was I a nigga when no matter what you said or did I was by your side, sayin' "Go Jelly Man. I'm wit'cha all the way." *(He grabs Jelly)* Call me a nigga again, n' I'm gonna kick your ass.

He exits into the void.

JELLY: Jack please . . . please . . .

SCENE 4

Central Avenue

The rhythms of jitterbug and early bebop fill the air as Jelly finds himself thrown into the garish neon world of Central Avenue. Lights reveal three Zoot Suiters and the Hunnies with nurse's hats and sunglasses—messengers of death.

CROWD:
DO-DO DO-DO
CENTRAL A-VE-NEW
DO-DO DO-DO
CENTRAL A-VE-NEW
DO-DO DO-DO
CENTRAL A-VE-NEW AH-AHHH

Chimney Man, the essence of Forties' hipster, appears. Percussive underscore.

CHIMNEY MAN: Ooooh ease me, grease me Sweet Papa Jelly.
JELLY: This place—

CHIMNEY MAN: Whatsamattah Jelly? Don't like the new sounds goin' 'round on Central Avenue? It's where you wound up after you left Anita.

JELLY: I know what happens here.

CHIMNEY MAN: I realize L.A. is not exactly the best place to die. Hell, they've barely figured out how to treat the living, but we all gotta jam with Sweet Daddy Death.

HUNNIES:

TELL YO' MAMA
AIN'T COMIN' HOME TONIGHT

CHIMNEY MAN: It all starts with an argument—

CROWD (Men):

STAB—STAB

Jelly is being taunted by three Zoot Suiters with knives and the Hunnies wearing nurse's caps.

CHIMNEY MAN: N' ends with you wastin' away in the Colored Wing of Los Angeles County General.

HUNNIES:

COME ON IN
WHERE YOU BEEN

JELLY *(Cowering; scared)*: Don't you touch me. Don't touch . . .

HUNNIES:

COME ON IN
WHERE YOU

Just when Jelly is about to be stabbed, Chimney Man halts the action.

CHIMNEY MAN: Better yet, let's skip all that n' get to my favorite part, you givin' up the ghost.

JELLY: I can't die. Not now. I've got to tell Jack. . . . N' Anita . . . n' . . .

CHIMNEY MAN:

NOOOOWWW!!!

On the Chimney Man's signal, Jelly releases a silent howl.

SCENE 5

The Last Rites

Percussive explosion. Lights reveal the Procession of the Dead, an otherworldly New Orleans/African parade of death coming to claim Jelly's soul.

The Chimney Man, who is carrying a large broom, "sweeps" and the Procession swirls around Jelly. He cowers in fear. When Jelly looks up, the Procession is gone and standing over him is Gran Mimi—tossing rose petals onto Jelly, as if he's in his grave.

GRAN MIMI:

BOY PRETTY BOY
NEVER GAVE YOU MY LOVE
BOY PRETTY BOY
NEVER GAVE YOU ANY LOVE
WHEN YOU GET NO LOVIN'
YOU GOT NO LOVIN' TO GIVE

The people and voices of Jelly's life fill the stage.

JACK: Was I a nigga when we wuz on the road together?
ANITA: So after all this time that's all I am to you?
CROWD *(A trio):*

FROM HIGH-FALUTIN' TO A HOLE IN THE GROUND

MISS MAMIE: Ooh darlin', my story lasted about as long as
   my song.

BUDDY: That's like wakin' up in the morning knowin' you
   gonna be alive at the end of the day.

SAM: For a yella runt—

AL: Sign the contract!

HUNNIES: You think they're bad—

HUNNIES ONE & TWO: Oooooooh Daddy!	ENSEMBLE *(Chants):* JAM!
CROWD MEMBER THREE: Dance all night to that Chicago Stomp . . .	JAM! JAM!

*The vocal cacophony continues to build as the Ensemble
hurls at Jelly the insults and slurs he's uttered all night.*

NORA: No coon stock in this Creole.	ENSEMBLE *(Chants):* JAM!
SAM: Be a good nigga n' put on the coat.	JAM!
CROWD MEMBER SEVEN: The only thing "shine" on me is the diamond in my tooth.	JAM! JAM! JAM!
CROWD MEMBER FIVE: I invented jazz.	JAM!
JACK: The only thing a nigga can do for me is scrub my steps and shine my shoes.	JAM! JAM! JAM!
BRICK-DUST LADY/HUNNIE TWO: Was I a nigga— Was I a nigga—	JAM! JAM! JAM!

*As the voices overlap and build to a peak, Jelly lets out
a cry.*

JELLY:
OHHH NO MORE
I SEE . . . I SEE

The Crowd fades into the void and Jelly is left alone.

SONG: CREOLE BOY/FINALE

JELLY:
CREOLE BOY GOES OUT ONE DAY
THINKIN' AIN'T HE SOMETHIN'
BRAG LIKE NUTHIN' YOU SEEN
BIG-TIME TALKIN' MACHINE
YEAH WELL LIVIN' IS MEAN
ALL THOSE FANCY SUITS YOU OWN
CREOLE BOY YOU STILL ALONE

CREOLE BOY SAYS "STEP ASIDE!
I GOT SOMETHIN' SPECIAL"
HIGH-TONE TALK ABOUT FAIR
HIGH-CLASS NOSE IN THE AIR
HEY, DON'T NOBODY CARE
CREOLE AIRS OR OTHERWISE
YOU STILL A NIGGER IN THEIR EYES

HE LIKES TO HANG WITH WHATCHA
MIGHT CALL LOW
UP WHERE THE BLUES IS BLOWIN'
MEAN N' SLOW
DOWN N' DARK AIN'T IN HIS JAM
"NO COON STOCK, HEY!
JE SUIS CREOLE
THAT'S WHAT I AM"
THE KING OF SWEET-ASS

SYNCOPATION
AIN'T NO BLACK NOTES IN MY SONG

(Music fil!)

JELLY:

I WAS WRONG

CREOLE BOY ONCE WAY BACK WHEN
HAD THE WHOLE WORLD SINGIN'
HAD THIS SOUND IN HIM, HEY!
A PAIN TOO HEAVY TO SAY
A PAIN HE STARTED TO PLAY
INSIDE EVERY NOTE OF HIS
IS WHAT HE CAME FROM . . . WHO HE IS

INSIDE EVERY NOTE OF HIS
IS WHAT HE CAME FROM . . . WHO HE IS

As Jelly continues to sing, lights reveal Miss Mamie and Buddy.

MISS MAMIE/BUDDY:

WE ARE THE RHYTHMS
THAT COLOR YOUR SONG

JELLY:

YOU ARE MY SONG.

Lights reveal Jack, Anita and Gran Mimi.

GRAN MIMI:

THE PAIN THAT MAKES THE MELODY STRONG

JELLY:

YOU ARE MY SONG . . .

JACK/ANITA/MISS MAMIE/BUDDY/GRAN MIMI

WE ARE THE FEELING

ENSEMBLE:

WE ARE THE FEELING IN YOUR SONG

The People from His Past envelop him. As they sing, the Yoruba door and the "shaft of darkness" leading to it, from the top of the show, appear. Jelly begins his ascent to the door, leaving the People from His Past behind.

ENSEMBLE:

ALL THE LYIN'
THE NEEDIN'
THE USIN'

JELLY:

THEY ARE MY SONG

ENSEMBLE:

ALL THE CRYIN'
THE BLEEDIN'
THE BRUISIN'

JELLY:

MY GLORIOUS SONG

Jelly exits through the door.

ENSEMBLE:

ALL THE LOVIN'
THE LEAVIN'
THE LOSIN'
WHO WE ARE
AND WHAT WE USED TO BE
IT'S IN THE MUSIC
PLAY THE MUSIC FOR ME . . .

*There is an instrumental explosion as lights reveal Jelly
followed by a New Orleans Funeral Band, complete
with "second liners," banners, images from his past—a
celebration which builds until Jelly is bathed in glorious
light.*

ENSEMBLE:

IT'S IN THE MUSIC

The Chimney Man appears.

CHIMNEY MAN:

Go forth Armstrong!
Go forth Ellington!
Go forth Basie, Bolden, n' Bechet!
Go forth Morton!

ENSEMBLE:

PLAY THE MUSIC FOR ME!

*The Funeral Band and "second liners" fade into the
void. Jelly is left alone, the faint sound of piano riffs in
the background.*

   *Jelly dances and mimes playing the piano until there
is . . .*

Blackness